Oriental Rugs
Care and Repair

Majid Amini

Oriental Rugs
Care and Repair

Macdonald Orbis

This book is dedicated to
the generations of unknown oriental rug
weavers, whose works are bought and sold as
masterpieces all over the world. In their
creators' lifetimes these fine works of art
brought them small praise and
little thanks.

A Macdonald Orbis BOOK

©Majid Amini 1981

First published in Great Britain in 1981
by Orbis Publishing Ltd

This edition published in 1987
by Macdonald & Co (Publishers) Ltd
London & Sydney

A member of BPCC plc

British Library Cataloguing in Publication Data
Amini, Majid
    Oriental rugs.
    1. Rugs, Oriental — Conservation and restoration
    I. Title
    746.7'5' 0288   NK2808

ISBN 0-356-14419-4

Printed and bound in Singapore by Toppan Printing Co Ltd

Macdonald & Co (Publishers) Ltd
Greater London House
Hampstead Road
London NW1 7QX

*Title page: a woman weaving at Shahsavan,
a winter village in the Hashtrud district of north-west
Iran. The long, narrow strip of warp-faced fabric is later
cut into equal lengths and sewn up to form various kinds
of domestic coverings.*

*Back cover: Ardibil Persian Carpet.
The Victoria and Albert Museum London/
The Bridgeman Art Library.*

Contents

Introduction

In the Orient, the art of traditional rug weaving is taught to children at a very early age (generally between the ages of five and seven). This is not done with a view to exploiting child labour, but is considered to be a part of the essential education of any child – just as in the West many children are encouraged to learn a musical instrument, or to take an interest in ballet or painting. With this life-enhancing object in view, the young oriental mind is exposed to all facets of rug making: its historical background, the elementary techniques of knotting, the appreciation of subtle blends of colour, the power and balance of visual design, the symbolism inherent in the motifs used and the unending patience needed.

People in the East are not alone in their deep-rooted love and appreciation of oriental rugs, for many people in the West also value the great contribution made by rug weavers to world culture. They treasure their rugs and respect them; they use them and enjoy them and they want to take care of them yet, sadly, many of these rugs and masterpieces of art often fall into neglect. This is not wilful neglect, but the result of a basic lack of elementary knowledge regarding the care and first-aid needed by handmade rugs. Rug owners often take no action at the first signs of wear, or worse still, they ruin their rug by attempting to use their own amateur methods of repair. Most people have probably seen the results of such untutored actions – antique rugs washed in an everyday washing machine and dried to a lustreless rag by a tumble dryer; silk rugs ruined with dirt and grease after years of use on a kitchen floor; fine old rugs with a part cut out to accommodate a jutting fireplace, and so on. The sight of these once beautiful and valuable rugs is pitiful. Yet, these disasters are brought about by rug lovers who do not know any better and who are unaware of the various ways in which their rugs could be protected, maintained and, if necessary, repaired at home.

Efforts in the past to seek advice on the care and maintenance of rugs have often proved fruitless. I am not aware of the existence of any specialized books on the subject and such short references as occur in journals or general rug books can even be misleading, giving damaging recommendations, such as the daily use of a powerful vacuum cleaner, nailing a rug to a staircase or gluing a rug to the floor to prevent it from moving. It is hoped that some of these misguided recommendations of the past can be rectified in this book, which is meant basically as a practical guide on the care and maintenance of oriental rugs. The text is aimed at one and the same time at the dealer, collector and investor, and also at the layman who has no specialized knowledge of the subject but a great love of oriental rugs.

As the art of rug weaving is slowly dying, a practical guide on the care of rugs is needed now more than ever before. Fewer and fewer rugs are available and those that

As part of her artistic education, this shy little girl is 'piling up' an Isfahan rug.

are deserve the same respect and attention given to any work of art. Correct care and maintenance will keep a rug in good condition, lengthen its useful life, assure its increasing investment value and enable it to be enjoyed and used by the generations to come.

Each handmade rug is unique; it is an individual creation of an artist and craftsman. The genius who creates a rug has to follow up his initial concept with months, and sometimes years, of hard and patient work to embody his moment of inspiration. Thus, every rug stands as a testimony to the infinite care, enthusiasm, skill and pleasure of an often unknown artist who may have worked far away in a different age and place and yet whose aesthetic values can still be vividly experienced and shared today. It is hoped that this book may serve to further the preservation of this testimony.

Majid Amini

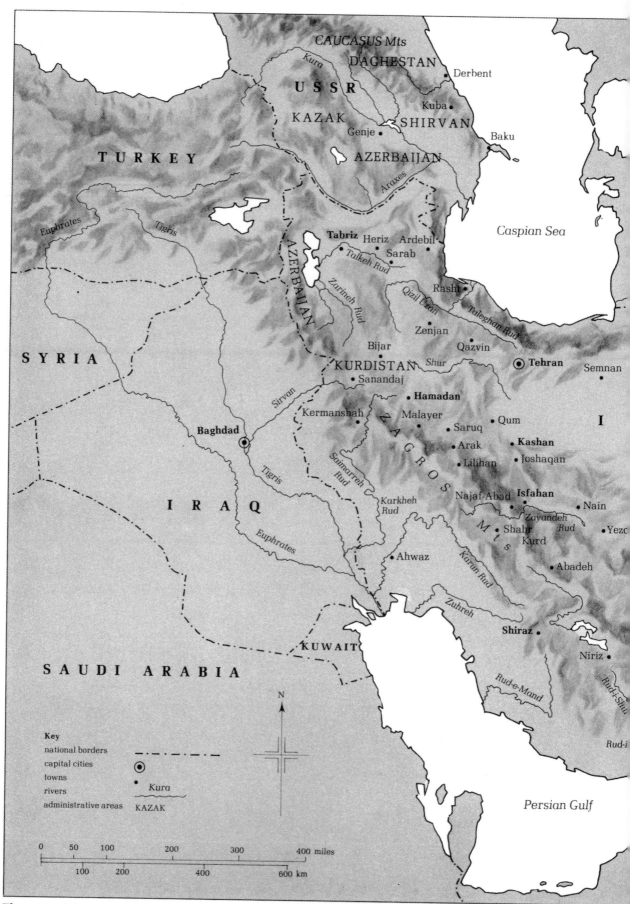

The principal rug-weaving areas of the world.

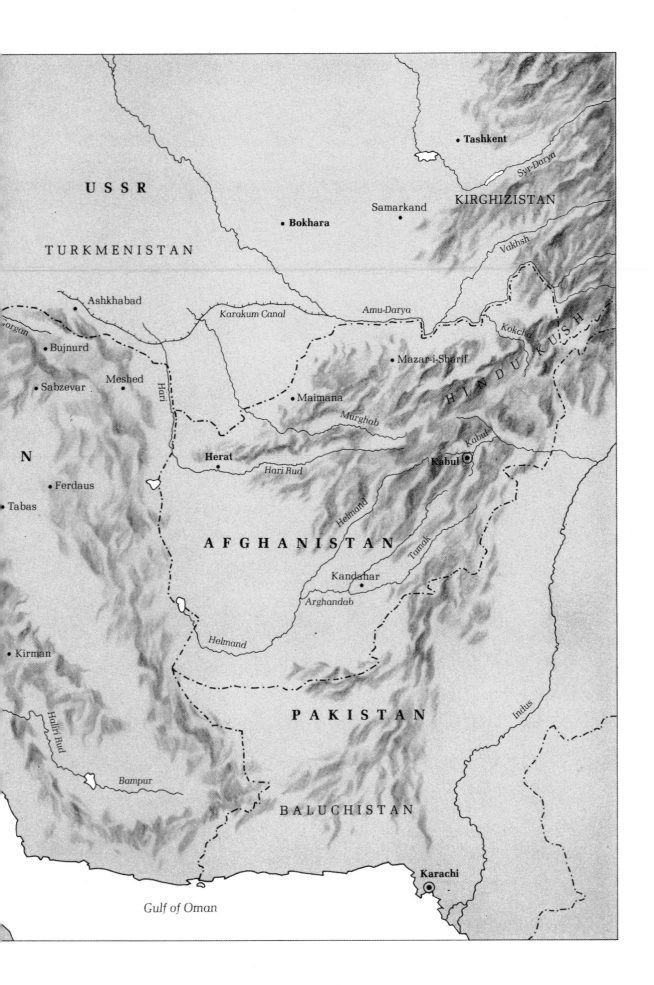

USSR

TURKMENISTAN

• Tashkent

KIRGHIZISTAN

Samarkand
•

• Bokhara

Syr-Darya

Vakhsh

Ashkhabad
•

Karakum Canal

Amu-Darya

Kokcha

HINDU KUSH

• Bujnurd

• Mazar-i-Sharif

organ

Hari

• Sabzevar

Meshed
•

• Maimana

Murghab

N

Kabul

• Ferdaus

Herat

Hari Rud

Kabul ⦿

• Tabas

Helmand

AFGHANISTAN

Tamak

• Kirman

Kandahar
•

Arghandab

Helmand

Haliri Rud

PAKISTAN

Indus

Bampur

BALUCHISTAN

Karachi ⦿

Gulf of Oman

Part I
Understanding Your Rug

Although oriental rugs can be appreciated simply for their splendid colours and designs, some understanding of their history, technique and classification can greatly enrich the rug owner's enjoyment. Beginning with a brief history of rug weaving, this section presents a basic cultural and technical background to the rug weaver's art.

Early seventeenth-century Mogul miniature showing the Emperor Babur (1483–1530) receiving nobles on a floral patterned carpet.

A History of Rug Weaving

The majority of books on oriental rugs begin with a scholarly and usually lengthy chapter on classic rugs and the history of rug making. This book, however, is primarily a practical manual and will confine itself to a brief glance at the subject.

Ancient man, who lived perhaps 20,000 years or more ago, gained his livelihood by hunting or trapping wild animals. For his protection and warmth he learned to use animal skins as clothing, as a barrier to the winds at the entrance to his cave, as ground and bedding covers and as containers. Later, he learned the art of animal husbandry and kept horses, oxen, goats and sheep. Then he compressed wool from some of these animals into felt or spun it into yarn. Fabrics would be woven from the yarn, out of which articles of clothing, blankets, floor coverings and bags would have been made. These were flat-woven fabrics and their invention was not the monopoly of any one region or ethnic group in the world.

The development of wool textiles with a piled surface woven into a foundation of warp and weft threads, was a later development that marked the emergence of a more sophisticated culture. Our present knowledge of the history of rug making is still in its infancy and it is not certain where and when such a step was first taken.

Unfortunately, wool textiles oxidize and crumble with the passage of time and, with one outstanding exception, no rugs dating before medieval times have survived to the present day. The exception is the famous Pazyryk rug, now in the Hermitage Museum in Leningrad in the Soviet Union. This rug measures 6 feet 7 inches by 6 feet (200 cm by 182 cm) and was excavated from a frozen tumulus in the Pazyryk valley, high in the Altai Mountains some six miles (9.5 km) inside the Soviet border with Mongolia. The Pazyryk rug was buried in a secondary chamber, thus protecting it from plundering thieves; it was successively flooded and then held in the grip of a permafrost until it was discovered, miraculously preserved, in 1947.

There is argument among scholars as to the precise age and origin of the Pazyryk rug, but it is reasonably certain that it was made between the second and fifth centuries before Christ. Many experts attribute the rug to early Persian weavers but it may possibly have been made by steppe nomads.

The Pazyryk rug is a remarkably powerful work of art. The design, simply drawn and finely executed, consists of a central rectangle divided into twenty-four squares, each square containing a cruciform motif not unlike that found as the secondary motif in modern Turkoman rugs. The central rectangle is enclosed by two principal borders, one containing a continuous line of twenty-four elks and the other a procession of twenty-eight warriors on horseback or walking beside their mounts. Separating the field and the main borders are a number of minor borders and guard stripes all woven with great delicacy.

This ancient relic confirms that, incredible as it may seem, little has changed in basic rug making over as much as a twenty-five century period. It also shows that, aesthetically, the impact of rugs is best conveyed by skilled draftsmanship and simplicity of design.

Little is known of the development of rug weaving over the next 1500 years. Certainly, the craft spread throughout Asia and the Middle East, through Turkey and up into the Caucasus, along North Africa and into Spain. From these countries, differing types of weaving emerged. Nomadic tribesmen wove rugs for their own domestic use. Rugs were also made in villages and weaving became a cottage industry with scope for making larger and also more delicate rugs; these rugs might be bartered or traded with travelling merchants. Large towns sprang up and the most skilful weavers gravitated towards them. Here, with the encouragement of merchants, rug making became an industry and weavers were organized in groups to supply custom works of art to order, often woven with the finest silks. Finally, powerful rulers, anxious to encourage the arts and thereby enhance their personal prestige, set up court workshops in which magnificent rugs were woven for the palace;

some of the greatest artists of the time designed such rugs.

After the Pazyryk rug, the most important landmarks in the history of rugs are the fragments excavated in East Turkestan by Sir Aurel Stein and dated to the second century; fragments excavated in Fostat (Old Cairo) attributed to the ninth and tenth centuries, and the famous 'Seljuk' rugs attributed to thirteenth- and fourteenth-century Anatolia, now in museums in Istanbul and Konya. With few exceptions, Turkish rugs of the fourteenth and early fifteenth centuries and Persian rugs made before the end of the fifteenth century are known only from paintings. A number of fifteenth- and sixteenth-century groups of Turkish rugs are indeed still called after such

Detail of the celebrated Pazyryk rug, excavated under the direction of the Soviet archaeologist, S. I. Rudenko, in the Altai mountain range. The outer, major border depicts cavalry horses with plaited tails. On the inner, major border of the rug grazing elks amble along in the opposite direction.

artists as Holbein and Lotto, in whose paintings they appear. There are examples of many different oriental rugs which were exported to Western Europe certainly from the fourteenth century and perhaps from periods following the Crusades. A small fragment of such a rug, dating from the fourteenth century, is now in New York's Metropolitan Museum.

Sixteenth-century Persia saw the dawning of the Golden Age of rug making. The impetus for its development was provided by the personal interest of the ruling monarchs of the Safavid dynasty who reigned from 1501 to 1736. Most famous for their patronage of the master weavers and for the establishment of court factories, were Shah Tahmasp I (who reigned from 1524 to 1576) and Shah Abbas I (1587–1629). It was during this period that the splendid baroque palace rugs were created which are now housed in the world's most prestigious museums. Many of these rugs were commissioned works. A famous example of a rug of this period is the Ardebil rug, from the Mosque of Ardebil, which is now in the Victoria

A Family Group, painted in 1547 by Lorenzo Lotto (c. 1480–1556), showing one of the many types of 'kufic' rug border.

Opposite: the Ardebil carpet, one of a pair of Persian medallion carpets bearing dates before AD 1600.

and Albert Museum in London. This formidable example of craftsmanship measures 36 feet 6 inches by 17 feet 6 inches (1112 cm by 533 cm), contains approximately thirty-two million knots and bears the date 946 AH (AD 1539–40). The significance of the date 946 AH is explained on page 53 which deals with the Islamic calendar and dated oriental rugs.

The art of rug weaving in Persia began to decline from the second half of the seventeenth century as the country became involved in successive wars with the Turks. This decline was largely in the area of rugs commissioned for the court, and rug weaving in the towns was not curtailed. This declining trend, accelerated

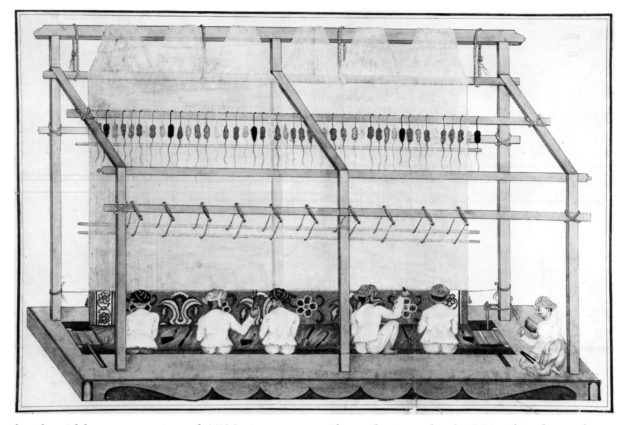

by the Afghan occupation of 1722, was not reversed until the foundation of the Qajar dynasty by Agha Mohammed in 1794. In Turkey rug-weaving showed no such break.

In the seventeenth and early eighteenth century rugs were made in the Caucasus, including the famous Dragon rugs. Distinguished pieces were also woven during this period in eastern Turkestan and possibly in China.

With the eclipse of the great Persian palace rugs, the tradition of weaving was carried on into the nineteenth century by nomads and village craftsmen in Persia. In the nineteenth century quality and artistic merit started to recover and the manufacture of pile rugs began to prosper as trading links developed with the rich areas of industrial Europe. Trading reached its peak in the late part of the century but, by the end of the century, rug production in many areas of Persia began to decline due to over-commercialization and the advent of the first chemical dyes. Nevertheless, good and sometimes excellent rugs have been made in the twentieth century. As Persia industrialized, inevitably the output of all handmade rugs in the traditional areas declined. Industry, mechanization and prosperity have enticed the weavers from their looms. The discovery of oil

Above: drawing, dated 1850, of a pile-carpet loom in use at Hunsur, southern India.

Opposite: antique Caucasian Dragon rug (10 ft×6 ft/305 cm×182 cm).

in Iran effected a complete change; many one-time weavers became employed by the oil and other industries at excellent hourly wages.

Rugs are still being made in most of the established rug-weaving countries, but the production of rugs of high artistic merit is limited. Needless to say, the price of such works, when available, is high and the law of supply and demand is pushing prices ever higher.

Today, hand-knotted rugs of varying quality are made on a commercial basis in many areas including India, Pakistan, Rumania, China and Bulgaria. Although rugs from these areas are not comparable with those of the past, they are playing an important role in the market today, giving the rug lover a chance to own and enjoy a handmade rug at a reasonable price.

The picture of world rug weaving that emerges from a study of the last five hundred years is, therefore, one of high quality, followed by occasional minor peaks and revivals to a decline both in quality and number.

The Technical Background

*B*asic techniques of rug weaving in the Orient have not changed for many centuries, even the looms and the tools have advanced little. Few mechanical devices, as we know them in the West, have been introduced, the hand-weaver's most sophisticated piece of machinery remaining a pair of scissors. The exceptionally high level of craftsmanship achieved with simple tools makes the oriental rug one of the most sought-after folk-arts.

The Material

The traditional material of the oriental rug is sheep's wool, although goat hair and camel hair have been used in a limited way by tribal weavers. Traditionally cotton has not been used extensively for the pile of rugs, although it is sometimes found in older rugs, especially in small areas of white pile and, in some types of rugs, in the wefts and, less frequently, in the warps. On the other hand, silk rugs have been highly regarded in the Orient from the earliest times. Some of the world's most famous sixteenth-century Persian rugs were made in silk and today silk remains the material used for the most prestigious and expensive modern rugs made in Persia and Turkey.

In the terminology of rug weaving, the yarn or thread consists of one or more strands of spun fibres. The way the yarn is formed is often characteristic to a particular weaving area and can be a useful identifying feature.

The Loom

All handmade rugs are made on a loom which supports the foundation of the rug into which the pile is knotted. Two types of loom are in use in the Orient: the horizontal or flat loom and the vertical or upright loom.

The flat loom consists of two wooden beams which are secured to the ground by strong ropes and pegs, similar to tent supports. The flat loom is mainly used by the nomadic or semi-nomadic weaver since it is easily transportable. Flat loom rugs are often uneven in shape, sometimes varying noticeably in width from one end of the rug to the other.

The upright loom is similar to the flat loom but is secured in the vertical position by two posts at either side of the beams. Both these looms have two wooden rods running across them horizontally — the heddle rod and the shed stick. This type of loom is stationary and is, therefore, used by village and town weavers, either in the workshop or in the home. It is not uncommon to find two upright looms set up opposite one another to produce a pair of rugs to the same design. Rugs made on vertical looms are more accurately dimensioned and more precise in drawing than those made on flat looms. The technique of knotting the rug is the same for both looms.

The Warp

The warp forms the base or 'foundation' upon which the rug is knotted. It consists of a series of parallel vertical threads (the warp threads) stretched taut around the two beams of the loom. The number of warp threads strung on the loom determines the fineness of weave, for instance an Isfahan rug may have between thirty and forty warp threads per inch (2.5 cm), whereas an Afghan rug may only have eight to twelve warps per inch (2.5 cm).

At the end of the rug the warp forms the foundation for the flat-woven 'kilim' which is provided as a protective — and sometimes decorative — end finish. At the ends of the kilim, the warp threads provide the fringes.

Much of the durability of the rug depends on the strength of the warp, hence strong, coarse wool is often used for the warp threads. In most older nomadic and village rugs as well as in many town workshop rugs, the warp threads are of undyed ivory- or brown-coloured wool. In some areas like Kirman, Hamadan and Najaf-Abad cotton is used and its use has tended to increase in rugs made

Two young Baluchi women weaving a kharari or floor cover at Kakrand, Sind, Pakistan. Baluchi weavers do not usually plan patterns using sketches, but work from memory, occasionally referring to an old fragment of cloth.

this century. Goat-hair warps are found in a smaller proportion of tribal rugs (for example, among those made by the Baluchi tribe and by some other weavers in Afghanistan). Silk warps are used for most silk pile rugs and in a few very fine antique woollen rugs. Silk fringes are the strongest of all and are used in finely knotted rugs such as those from Isfahan.

19

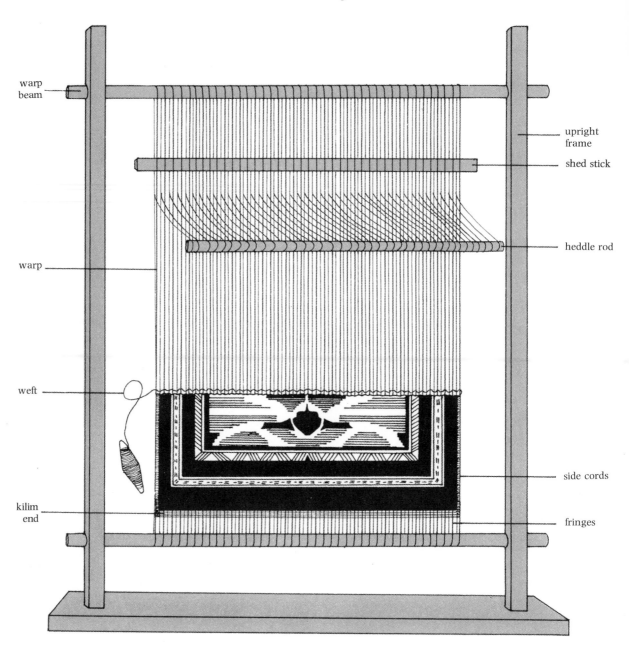

Example of a vertical or upright loom showing the basic construction of a rug.

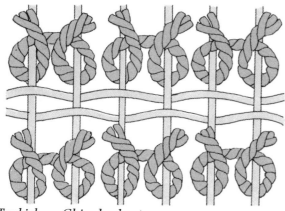

Turkish or Ghiordes knots.

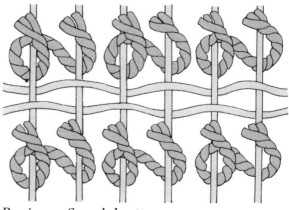

Persian or Senneh knots.

The Weft

The weft shots, shoots or shotz pass horizontally in and out of the warp threads. This is achieved by means of the heddle rod and the shed stick. The heddle rod is attached to alternate warp threads by means of loops and as it is raised half the warps are raised creating a shed through which the weft shoots can be threaded. Then the shed stick, which separates other alternate warp threads, and is situated by the warp beam (furthest from the weaver) is moved, providing a counter shed through which other wefts can be threaded. The first part of the rug to be woven is a length of 'kilim' (weft-faced plain-weave) and a similar finish is applied to the other end to complete the rug. The kilim end acts as a firm guard which prevents the rug from fraying. In urban rugs, the kilim ends are normally between $1\frac{1}{2}$ inches to $\frac{1}{16}$ inch (1.5–38 mm) in length. In tribal rugs, for example, those woven by Kurdish, Turkoman or Baluchi weavers, long kilm ends may provide a decorative feature at the ends of the pile.

In the piled part of a rug, the wefts provide support for the knots. After completing a row of knots, the weaver passes one or more weft shots in and out of the warp threads, then beats the fabric down by hand using a heavy metal comb. The wefts hold the knots in place and their number and thickness also determine the vertical knot count of the rug. Thus in some tribal rugs made in Persia, as well as in some Caucasian and North African rugs, multiple wefts are provided to separate the rows of knots and thus to give vertically steeper designs, often, however, at the cost of producing a looser, less durable weave.

In most tribal and village rugs, the wefts are of wool, less frequently of cotton, although, as in the case of the warps, the use of cotton has increased in some areas during this century. Cotton wefts are not necessarily an indication of recent production, however. In a number of early Persian and Chinese carpets cotton was the traditional weft material and some early Turkoman rugs have cotton or mixed wool and cotton wefts. Woollen wefts in many Persian, Turkish and some Caucasian rugs are often dyed, mainly in a shade of red; in other Caucasian rugs and in most Turkoman rugs, they are of undyed ivory or brown wool. Silk wefts are found not only in silk-pile rugs but in some finely woven wool-pile rugs.

The total weft thickness is determined not only by the thickness of the yarn but by the number of strands used to form the weft shot (normally one or two in woollen wefts, two or three in cotton wefts and multiple strands in silk wefts) and by the number of shots passed between the rows of knots. Two shots are normal for most rugs but single-wefted fabrics are found in tribal as well as urban rugs. In some Persian rugs, for example, those made in Kirman in the south and in Bijar in the west, three weft shots are provided in which two outer shots are given a different degree of tension to the inner to provide a two-level 'depressed' foundation.

'Depression'

While many rugs are woven with the weft shots passing between the warp threads in a regular manner, producing a flat fabric, in others, extra tension is applied to one or more of the weft shots in such a way that alternate warp threads are displaced vertically, forming a two-level foundation on which the two lobes of the knot are placed at an angle. In extreme cases, one of the warps of a pair may lie directly above the other, so that from the back of the rug, only one of the two ridges is visible. Such rugs are often said to have a 'depressed' structure and it is important to be aware of the presence or absence of depression both when determining the horizontal knot count and in deciding on the best method for restoring a damaged rug. In general, rugs with depressed structures are more difficult to repair. The degree of depression also serves as a useful identifying feature for different types of rugs.

In rugs with a Turkish (symmetric) knot, depression causes the pile to slant either to the left or the right, depending on the knotting technique. In Persian or asymmetrically knotted rugs, the slant of the pile is towards the direction in which the knot is open.

Side Cords or Selvedges

The sides of a rug are normally secured by a selvedge, formed from one or several warp threads, used singly or twisted together to form 'cables' which are bound by the weft shots to produce a cord. In other cases, the wefts are woven in and out of individual pairs of warps in a figure of eight which may be extended to form a flat, wide side finish. On many rugs, additional protection or decoration may be applied to the selvedge by an extra binding of wool in one or more colours. Information on the most common flat-weave structures is given in the chapter on classifying rugs.

The Knot

The knot is formed by tying the yarn, made of wool, cotton or silk, around two warp threads. It is then secured in position row by row by the weft. When a row of knots has been tied, it is trimmed to the desired length. Hand-knotting is a highly skilled operation and, in most rugs, it is carried out by women or young children since their smaller fingers can move more easily

between the narrowly spaced warp threads. In north-western Persia, however, a hook is used for knotting.

A rug may contain several million hand-tied knots. On average, a skilled weaver can tie about twenty-five knots per minute, completing 12,000 to 15,000 knots in a day. Thus, based on a fifty-hour week, it would take an experienced weaver about ten months to complete a rug measuring 9 feet by 12 feet (275 cm by 365 cm) which is tied with two hundred knots per square inch (about 3,000 knots per

Two simple outdoor looms set up under the eaves of a house in an Iranian village. The team of weavers on the right perches high above a geometric rug which is in the latter stages of completion.

22

dm² — one decimetre is equal to ten centimetres).

Knot density varies widely. Coarse rugs are made with knot densities as low as twenty-five knots per square inch (approximately 400 knots per cm²) while at the other end of the scale, very fine rugs, nomadic or urban, may have six hundred knots per square inch (approximately 9,500 knots per dm²). The finest knotted rug known is an Indian silk rug with about 2,500 knots per square inch (around 40,000 knots per dm²). Although fineness of knotting determines the labour element in a rug, and thus its price when new, it would be wrong to think that it determines the value of antique rugs. Many of the most valuable early rugs are quite coarsely knotted. When judging the fineness of knotting in an oriental rug it must be compared with another rug of the same type, quality, age and condition etc. It follows, therefore, that a finely knotted Pakistani rug is neither better nor more valuable than a coarsely knotted Kazak as they are two different things and cannot be compared.

Types of knots There are various ways of knotting a rug, but in the Orient there are mainly two types of knot used in making a rug by hand: the Persian or Senneh knot (also known as the asymmetric knot) and the Turkish or Ghiordes knot (also known as the symmetric knot). Persian knots may be open to the left or the right, looking at the rug with the pile slanting downwards, in other words with the end at which the rug was started at the bottom. The direction of the knot is sometimes a useful distinguishing feature between types of rugs.

To distinguish between rugs woven with the Persian and Turkish knot choose a vertical line of knots on the front of the rug, preferably at a place where a vertical design line is one knot wide, and with the pile pointing downward (with the direction of weaving from the bottom to the top). Fold the rug back from the line of knots on both sides and attempt to part the two threads which form the ends of the knot. If you cannot separate them, it is a symmetric knot. If you can part the two ends, showing a section of the warp underneath, you are looking at an asymmetric knot.

Other knot variations While in the great majority of oriental rugs, the Persian knot is tied over two warp threads, in a smaller number of rugs, it is tied over four warps. On some early Persian rugs, this method of tying the knot, called *jufti* knotting, had the purpose of evening out the horizontal to vertical count ratio, which directly affects the designs, of rugs with unusually low vertical knot counts. In some Persian rugs, mainly among those made in the early part of this century, *jufti* knotting was introduced as a time-saving device. In such a case it tended to produce an inferior structure with a markedly lower life-expectancy.

While in the great majority of rugs, the knots are tied row by row over the same pairs of warps, in some rugs, notably some Kurdish and North African rugs, the knots are offset or staggered by one warp thread, in other words the first loop of the knot is placed directly above the second loop of the knot below. The effect of this technique is to produce steeper diagonal designs and in some nomadic rugs, 'offset knotting' is used only in those areas of the rug in which the design requires it.

In a number of, mainly tribal, rugs, both Persian and Turkish knots are found. This is particularly common in a number of South Persian and Turkoman tribal rugs woven in the Persian knot in which one or more Turkish 'edge' knots are tied at the ends of each row in order to strengthen the sides. A different edge knot, so far thought to be unique to the Yomut Turkoman, is a characteristic variant of the Turkish knot.

In general, most rugs made in Persia, Egypt, China, India and East Turkestan, as well as modern Pakistani rugs, were made with the Persian knot. In the great majority of these the knot is open on the left, although most Turkoman rugs made with the Persian knot and some Persian rugs, have the knot open on the right.

The Turkish knot was used in almost all rugs made in Turkey and the Caucasus. However, it is also traditional in some areas of Persia, particularly in the north-west and in some tribal weaving areas in the south. Among Turkoman rugs, those made by the Saryk and the majority attributed to the Yomut are woven with the Turkish knot.

Design and Colour

Not only is the Pazyryk rug the oldest knotted rug which has survived; it is artistically one of the most successful rugs we know, and especially interesting because it combines two principles of decorative art: the naturalistic and the abstract. In the Pazyryk rug, the realistically drawn animal figures in the borders surround a geometric field composition, a vertical and horizontal repeat of cruciform ornaments in compartments.

Of the two principles, the abstract or geometric has proved to be the more important in the history of the oriental rug. Only in some of the Turkish rugs known to us from fourteenth- and fifteenth-century Western paintings, do we see animal figures dominating the field, and even in these their representation is stylized to the point where realism and abstract art meet. In many of the Persian rugs of the early Safavid period in the sixteenth century, we see semi-naturalistic mythological animal figures grouped around and subordinate to geometric ornaments. It is only in the twentieth century that 'pictorial' rugs, depicting scenes from Persian history or legend, or even from Western books, started to appear in Iran and rugs with portraits and scenes from post-revolutionary Russia began to be produced in the workshops of Soviet Turkmenistan. Many such rugs are technically excellent and command respect and, sometimes, high prices in their country of origin, but they are not part of the tradition of the oriental carpet. To say this is not to deny their artistic merit; they find their parallel in the textile picture of medieval and modern Western tapestries, but they belong to a different tradition which conforms to different laws.

The mainstream of the art of the oriental rug is closely identified with the Turkic tribes which migrated westward from eastern Asia during a period spanning two millennia. This essentially abstract art was adapted and refined by weavers working in many different local traditions, in workshops producing rugs for the courts and for the requirements of home and export markets in many different countries, as well as by tribal and village weavers making rugs for their own use in the house or in the tent. Over the many centuries through which the art of the rug in the rug-weaving countries can be traced, a number of periods of artistic flowering, of stagnation and resurgence as well as of decline can be identified, yet all these changes have taken place essentially within a firmly based tradition which dates back two and a half millennia.

Most oriental rug designs are based on the principle of the endless repeat in which the pattern is projected, apparently without end, in all four directions. The borders of the rug are an essential element; they form the counterpart of the field pattern, enclosing a section of the endless design and presenting it without setting bounds to it.

There are, of course, other design principles in the oriental rug; one of the most important is the concept of the centre medallion. In a simple medallion composition, the centre ornament acts as a unifying focus to the design, balanced by subsidiary ornaments which are grouped around it, orientated towards the corners of the rectangular field. By no means all medallion compositions, however, abandon the endless repeat; in many examples, quarter medallions, cut by the borders at the four corners, carry the illusion of continuity.

Major ornaments within endless repeat patterns are often surrounded by minor motifs, arranged in rhythmically repeating, regular or offset rows in which variety is given by simple or sometimes highly complex alternations of colour. Single ornaments or groups of ornaments are enclosed in compartment patterns or in diagonal lattices; subtle differences in shape, size or colour between ornaments, help to form larger combinations which, in turn are organized into repeats, echoing a basic design theme or creating complementary themes.

It is impossible to present, within the scope of this book, more than a few of the many examples of designs which make up the art of the oriental rug and which underlie the almost endless variety of patterns based on geometric ornament.

Rectilinear and Curvilinear Designs

Rectilinear design in which the ornaments are drawn in straight lines, is often contrasted with the less rigid curvilinear designs which reproduce curved outlines. Designs are drawn on rugs by colour changes executed on a grid which corresponds to the horizontal and vertical rows of knots. Hence a rug design cannot be drawn as a true curve but rather as a planned succession of vertical, diagonal and horizontal lines. To create the illusion of a curve generally requires the base of finely knotted weaving, rugs with low knot densities being adapted only for designs executed in straight lines. Nevertheless, a high knot density is not by any means always associated with curvilinear designs, equally important is the method by which the design is transmitted onto the rug. With some exceptions, tribal rugs, in which the designs are mainly copied 'free-hand' from other rugs, or in which the model exists in the memory, tend to embody rectilinear designs. In general, curvilinear designs are more intricate in detail and are produced from cartoons on which the pattern is reproduced knot by knot on squared paper, a technique which is more common in workshop production. It would be wrong to conclude from this that

An artist preparing a design for the patterned border of a Kashan rug using squared paper. Each square represents a single knot which the artist fills in with the colour the weavers are to follow.

curvilinear designs are superior or inferior to rectilinear ones; there are excellent and displeasing designs of both types.

Types of Design

There are many classic designs, often incorporating symbolic motifs, which date back for centuries. As it would be impossible to discuss all the designs in this book, the following interesting examples have been selected for detailed discussion.

Prayer rugs The prayer rug, or Namazlik as it is sometimes known, was first introduced for use by the Muslim who prays five times a day. His religion decrees that seven points of the body must touch a clean ground — the two knee caps, the forehead, the two big toes and the two palms of the hand. At the time of prayer, the Muslim turns his prayer rug to face the Holy City of Mecca, the birthplace of the Great Prophet Mohammed.

As rug weaving progressed and as bureaucracy intertwined with religion, so finer and

*A mid-to-late nineteenth-century Qashqā'i
rug displaying a triple medallion design
(8 ft 3 in×4 ft 11 in/251.6 cm×147.7 cm).*

*Opposite: antique Persian town rug woven to a
European design and bearing an unusually
elongated centre medallion.*

An antique silk Kashan Tree of Life rug.

A modern Isfahan Seirafian hunting rug.

more splendid rugs were executed to meet the demands of the ostentatious rich. The richer the Muslim, the more extravagant and opulent his prayer rug.

A prayer rug carries a token of the mosque in the form of an arch, sometimes known as the *mehrab* or niche, which should be pointed towards Mecca at the time of prayer. In some rugs the *mehrab* is curved and ornate (Kashan, Hereke, Tabriz), whereas in most tribal rugs it is more angular (Baluchi, Bokhara, Beshir).

Most prayer rugs are very alike in the basic concept, having a niche as the principal dominating design. However, as each tribe or area has its own particular characteristics, it is not difficult to recognize the origins of the work. The most common prayer rugs from urban regions are Turkish (Melez, Ghiordes, Ladik, Hereke, Kayseri); Persian (Tabriz, Kashan, Isfahan, Qum, Sarouk); and the Caucasus (Daghestan, Kazak, Shirvan, Fachralo, Marasali). Tribal prayer rugs are primarily made by the Baluchi, Kurds, Shiraz, Turkomans and Baktiari.

As with most religions, the community spirit is encouraged by the Muslims and as a

result multiple prayer rugs were also introduced for use by all the family. These rugs may comprise two or more complete prayer designs woven into one rug. These rugs, which are often seen in Arabian mosques, are also known as *saphs* and emanate mainly from Turkey and Persia.

The design of prayer rugs opened a new artistic chapter in rug weaving, introducing more intricate patterns with great richness of colour and precise execution. They have proved so popular in both East and West for decorative purposes that now many non-Muslim weavers, such as Armenians in the Caucasus, are producing them.

Tree of Life rugs The origin of the Tree of Life design varies between races and countries. To the Jews, the Tree of Life (or Tree of Knowledge of Good and Evil) grew in the Garden of Eden; the Muslims believe that it grew in Paradise; and the Chinese are taught that it came from the Sea of Jade. To all the basic significance remains the same — eternal life.

The design is executed in various ways,

28

according to the culture and tradition of the weaver. In some rugs the Tree of Life is depicted as a single tree with branches and flowers. Sometimes it is seen as two trees with inter-twining branches, known as the double Tree of Life. Occasionally, the tree symbolism appears only as a bunch of flowers in a vase and when this motif is repeated across the field it is known as the *zil-i-soltan* design. In other rugs, only the leaves of the Tree of Life appear, filling the entire field. Some rugs from the Kirman area depict the Tree of Life as sur-rounded at its base by hills or perhaps moun-tains, in addition to animals.

Hunting rugs A typical and popular theme in Persian rugs is that of the hunt. Horses and hunting have played a great part in Persian life and it was the Persians themselves who invented the royal game of polo. Hunting rugs often depict the rider armed with weapons and in pursuit of wild animals (lions, gazelles or deer); sometimes the design only shows the mounted rider. Great examples of hunting rugs were woven in the sixteenth century but, amongst others, the towns of Qum, Tabriz, Kirman and Isfahan still continue to elaborate this vivid design.

Garden of Persia rugs The Garden of Persia is another classic and traditional design. It depicts a perfectly symmetrical garden which is divided into sections by a stream of cool water, in which swim small fishes, and the garden areas are filled with richly coloured flowers, cypress trees and bushes etc. Occa-sionally, animals are also featured. Again, magnificent examples of this design were woven in the sixteenth century, yet it con-tinues to be produced occasionally by the Baktiari tribes and the weavers of Qum.

Other Pictorial Rugs

Particularly in Persia, short stories, proverbs and poems by great writers have been painted by skilled artists as miniatures. These minia-tures have often found themselves enlarged and woven with great delicacy into rugs. Favourite subjects for pictorial rugs are taken from Omar Khayyam. Other pictorial rugs in-clude pastoral views, famous mosques, ac-claimed paintings or simply animal forms

An eighteenth-century Persian garden rug.

29

A Baluchi prayer rug in which the niche is decorated with a stylized Tree of Life design. The woven inscription calls on the names of God, Mohammed and his disciples.

Above: detail of a Tabriz silk pictorial rug in which the star-like design reflects the resplendent architectural detail of the ceiling of a mosque.

(camels and dogs etc). More recently in the Tehran and Istanbul bazaars, portraits of Islamic prophets or religious leaders, kings, heads of state, famous musicians and personalities have been on sale. These rugs are often technically excellent, although many of these designs may not always appeal to Western taste.

Natural and Symbolic Motifs

Ornaments from nature in the form of flowers, trees and animals, have always had a place in the geometric design tradition of the oriental carpet, the blend between the seemingly incompatible art principles being achieved by stylization and repetition of the natural forms. It is important to remember also that the oriental rug was made not only as a functional item, or even as a decorative object; in the Orient, art was not so strictly divorced from religion as it is in the West and the rug served as an aid to religious contemplation and thus reflected a traditional iconography which linked rug designs to ancient religious, cosmic and mythological concepts.

The symbolic designs in oriental rugs are on many different levels of sophistication. In the large rugs made for palaces and mosques in sixteenth-century Persia, the designs incorporated the iconography of Islam, interpreted by the great artists of the period. In the village rug, the symbolism is of a simpler kind, but always based on a concept of the relationship of man to nature which is deeply rooted in ancient realities and reflected in ancient myths. The symbolic content of rug ornaments is not, primarily, a picture language to be interpreted into Western language. Its meanings are recognized on the deeper levels of consciousness, in which occidental as well as oriental man has his roots.

Many basic motifs recur throughout the centuries, each reproduction of the theme individually varied and adorned by the weavers. Certain motifs have a particular symbolism, which frequently differs from one end of the country to the other. Many of these interesting motifs continue to be woven in the

Example of a typical twentieth-century lion rug made by the Qashqā'i tribe of Fars province in Iran. This type of rug is usually coarsely and loosely woven and is used to cover stacks of bedding or clothing.

32

twentieth century, the tradition having been passed from father to son for generations.

In Persia, some of the most recurring motifs with known representations are:

Cypress Tree Survival in the after-life

Tree of Life Eternal life

Pomegranates Riches in abundance

Camels Wealth and happiness

Peacock The sacred bird

Dove Peace and good omens

Comb Cleanliness, or sometimes, the Pillars of the Faith (the five pillars on which Islam rests)

Hour Glass A reminder that time runs out for all and that there is no escape

Cloud Bands Good fortune

Weeping Willow Death, sorrow, grief

Cock The devil, woven into the rug to protect the owner or user from the evil eye

Lions Victory and glory

Dogs To protect the owner or user from theft

Colours and Dyes

In oriental countries, a rug is often valued primarily for its colours and it is probably true to say that in the Western world, beauty of colour and colour combinations in rugs are influential factors. Colours communicate directly to man's aesthetic feelings; designs and ornaments of a rug are also perceived through colour contrasts. In a very real sense, therefore, colour and design are complementary features.

Colours are also important distinguishing features since rugs made in different areas differ greatly in the number of colours used and their shades. The connoisseur can often tell quite intuitively where an oriental rug was made by its characteristic colour combinations.

The dyes used to obtain the great variety of colour shades in the older oriental rugs are derived from plants, insects and, to some extent, from minerals. The synthetic dyestuffs on most modern rugs began to come into use soon after they were first introduced in the 1860s.

When the colours of a rug are discussed, it is usually the pile which is being referred to. However, in many rugs, particularly those from Turkey, but also a proportion of those made in Persia and the Caucasus, coloured (usually red) wefts were used, principally in order to blend in with the colour of the pile. Warps, on the other hand, were almost always left undyed.

The Meaning of Colours
To the people of the East, each and every colour has a traditional meaning. Green, for example, is considered by Muslims to be the holy colour, being the colour of the Prophet's coat. Although used in prayer rugs, green was, therefore, never used in decorative rugs as it is disrespectful to walk on the holy colour. At the end of the last century, however, Western demand, influenced by French art and taste, produced numerous rugs incorporating green for export — a case of piety being swept aside by a booming economy. Other examples of colour symbolism are:

Black Revolt, destruction
Brown Good harvest, fertility
White Purity and peace, as well as the colour of mourning
Gold Wealth and power
Yellow The Emperor's colour
Red Happiness and joy
Dark Blue Solitude, authority, power
Light Blue The heavenly colour, Iran's national colour and the colour of mourning.

Although this list has been included to give some idea of the symbolic weight of colours, it should be noted that most rug-weaving nations interpret the colours differently; and that such symbolism can even vary from north to south within one rug-weaving country.

Natural Dyes

By far the most important of natural red dyes is madder, derived from the root of *Rubia tinctorum*. Madder has been used for dyeing textiles from the time of ancient Egypt and by employing different preparation techniques, different concentrations and additives, its two principal constituents, alizarin and purpurin yield a vast range of shades, varying from pale orange to deep brown and purple. The lighter shades are often obtained by the admixture of a yellow plant dye, the darker by the effect of iron salts, mainly during mordanting (preparation of the wool for dyeing). Madder is used widely on wool, rarely, if ever, on silk.

Second in importance of the red dyes is the insect dye cochineal, derived from *Dactylopius coccus*, which was introduced from the American continent early in the sixteenth century and which came into use in the dif-

Above: a wool dyer immersing skeins of virgin wool in dye vats where they will be left to simmer for several hours. The sodden wool is then hung over wooden frames to dry.

Opposite: this Sarouk rug, made at the turn of the century, clearly shows abrash, or dye change.

ferent oriental rug-producing countries, probably from the late eighteenth to the mid-nineteenth century. The active constituent is carmenic acid and it now seems likely that the same ingredient is present in one or more other insect dyes used before cochineal was imported in Persia and Central Asia.

Another insect dye, lac, derived from *Laccifer lacca* was used widely in India since ancient times and is found in Indian carpets up to the nineteenth century, in Safavid Persian

carpets and in some early Turkoman pieces. Both cochineal and lac give deep red and bluish-red shades and are often difficult to distinguish visually. Lac is found most often on wool, cochineal on both wool and silk.

Blue The only blue dye of importance is indigo, obtained from *Indigofera tinctoria*, and mainly imported from India to all the rug-producing countries. Indigo is also unique among the plant dyes used in oriental rugs in that it can be economically synthesized; it is not generally possible to distinguish between natural and synthetic indigo. Indigo has been used on wool, silk and cotton.

Yellow A very large number of dye plants were apparently used for obtaining yellow shades and it is only very recently that chemical analysis methods have been perfected which can distinguish effectively between them. Among the most common of these, weld, is

Sorters at work in a wool warehouse in Iran in which the subtly differing shades of natural wool, ranging from near-white to deep ivory, are being sorted ready for the dyeing process.

found in rugs made in a large area from Turkey to East Turkestan while for many Persian and Central Asian rugs yellow was obtained from a plant known by the name *isparuk* or *esbaruk*, thought to be a *Delphinium* species. However, there were undoubtedly many other plants in use for yellow dyes. In many rugs, a little madder has been found mixed with the yellow dye, to give brighter shades.

Green Shades of many different depths of green were invariably obtained by double-dyeing with indigo and one of the yellow dyes.

Brown Natural brown wool has been used traditionally for outlines of ornaments in rugs from most areas. In some cases, as in many

Persian and Central Asian rugs, this is artificially darkened to black with iron salts. Natural brown camel hair is also found in some Persian and Baluchi rugs. Dyed shades of brown on older rugs were often obtained with madder, darkened with iron. Other brown shades were probably in use but no reliable information has yet been obtained on these.

White (ivory) Almost invariably, white areas in rugs are natural sheep's wool in shades which range from almost pure white to dark ivory. In a relatively few rugs, light-coloured (beige) camel hair is used. Pure white shades are often made from cotton.

Synthetic Dyes

The first synthetic dyes came into use on oriental rugs in the 1860s, when the mauve dyestuff Fuchsine was introduced into the major rug-weaving areas. Fuchsine, however, proved to be a fugitive dye — it was not very fast in light and, because of this, soon fell into disrepute. While laws banning its use in Iran were often more honoured in the breach than in the observance, Fuchsine was superseded by improved dyes within a relatively short time and it is believed that it is contained in few rugs made after the 1890s. The presence of Fuchsine can often be seen in the base of the knots of faded areas of rugs dating from this period.

Synthetic dyes with improved light-fastness came into use from about the middle 1880s in the rug-weaving areas. Most important of these are the azo dyestuffs imported from Germany, England and Russia. The first of these to be introduced were a number of red dyes used to replace madder for specific shades and in rugs of the early synthetic dye period it is common to see just one red azo dye used in combination with the traditional plant and insect dyes. As the European chemical industry improved its dyes, more and more synthetic dyes were used in oriental rug production, until by the end of World War II, the use of natural dyes was limited to a few workshops and fewer tribal weavers.

Fastness to Light and Water

The different natural dyes derived from plants and insects fade at variable rates on exposure to light. Even natural brown sheep's wool fades in sunlight and, in general, all old oriental rugs need protection from excessive illumination. It is worth noting that the mellow shades of many antique rugs which are highly regarded in the West, very often had a totally different appearance when they were made. This can be seen from rare examples which have been stored in the dark for many decades or even centuries. Sometimes the bright colours of such rugs are as unfamiliar to Western eyes as a newly cleaned old master painting.

Among the least light-fast of natural dyes were some of the yellow plant dyes, which, in old rugs, have often faded to ivory. This also affects many green shades in old rugs in which the yellow has faded leaving the blue of the indigo. In less extreme cases, green has changed to a shade of turquoise. Such fading can often be observed by comparing the front of the rug with the back which has not been exposed to the same degree of light.

Apart from the first-generation synthetic dyes such as Fuchsine, most of the more recent dyes are relatively light-fast and oriental rugs made since World War II are not likely to change colour significantly with time. Because of their tendency to fade, valuable antique rugs in museums are often protected by strictly controlling the type and degree of illumination.

Water-fastness of dyes is important mainly in deciding how to clean a rug. Most plant and insect dyes used on old oriental rugs are relatively stable to water and do not run when a rug is cleaned. However, this depends both on the material and the method in which it has been prepared. Dyed silk tends to run more readily than wool containing the same natural dye. Poorly mordanted pile wool or wool which has been 'over-dyed' may run when a rug is cleaned, even after some centuries.

Most modern synthetic dyes are perfectly stable in cleaning, but earlier azo dyes on old rugs show variable water-fastness. A number of such dyes, including the ubiquitous red azo dye Ponceau 2R, widely used in Persia and Central Asia from the 1890s onward, is fairly stable although the dye may sometimes be seen to have stained the warps. At the other extreme, some dyes of this period, such as Rocceline, used in the same areas, will bleed if slightly moistened, many decades later.

As a result of soaking this rug with water, the unstable red dye has bled into the white areas of the design and blurred the pattern.

The same rug after the colour-run problem has been corrected by an expert. This treatment should be always left to professionals.

Before cleaning a rug (or giving it to be cleaned), it is best to test the dyes for colour fastness (details are given in the section on hand cleaning). Particular attention should be given to the red colours which are most likely to bleed, but preferably all the different shades should be tested. Silk rugs or woollen rugs with substantial areas of silk should never be cleaned without testing the dyes for colour-fastness. Tiny areas of silk, such as are found in some old rugs from central Asia, should be tested in the same way as the wool.

Abrash

Some rugs show marked and sharply defined shade differences within one colour. Such colour variations, which are called *abrash*, are not due to fading but to the use of successive batches of wool by the weaver which show slight or distinct variations in dyeing technique. *Abrash* is found more often in nomadic or village rugs; it is rare in town weavings. In some cases, such colour variations may be disturbing, but often they add charm.

Corrosion

Some old rugs show areas in which the dyed wool or silk has 'corroded' leaving the pile noticeably shorter than in adjacent areas. Wool which has been treated with iron salts in mordanting is particularly vulnerable to corrosion; this can be seen in rugs in which outlines of designs have been woven in natural brown wool which has been darkened with iron, and in wool or silk dyed with one of the insect dyes (see above). Where corrosion is slight, it will not detract from the appearance, but may even add an attractive 'relief' effect. In extreme cases, where the pile has corroded to the base of the knots, the area may require repiling.

Chemical Washing

Many modern oriental rugs are chemically 'washed', either in the country of origin or by specialist firms in the West, to change the original shades of colour. Chemical washing is a bleaching process in which a proportion of the dye is removed or chemically changed by the action of oxidizing or reducing agents. While such rugs may be acceptable furnishing pieces, they are avoided by collectors. Usually the purpose of using this process is to produce the more subdued shades preferred in Western countries; occasionally the colour is changed entirely, as where the normal red ground colour of some rugs made in Afghanistan is changed to a deep yellow to produce 'Golden Afghans' or in some modern Chinese rugs pastel shades are produced. However, some rugs made earlier this century have also been chemically washed; an example is provided by East Turkestan rugs (known in the trade as 'Samarkand') which were chemically washed, particularly for American sale.

Classifying Your Rug

The majority of rugs are made by anonymous weavers and are not signed as a painting is by its artist. However, each village or tribe in the very extensive rug-weaving areas of the world produces rugs with their own characteristic combination of designs and ornaments, colours and technical features. These characteristics help to define the specific origin of a rug. Design alone, however, is not enough; this is not only true of modern rugs where, for example, classical Persian and Caucasian designs are being reproduced by Indian and Pakistani weavers, but from the earliest periods, popular rug designs of one country have been taken up, with greater or smaller stylistic adaptations, by weavers in other areas. A great deal of experience and expertise is therefore required to attribute oriental rugs correctly; even knowledgeable specialists by no means always agree with one another. This is particularly true of the rarer types of antique rugs.

The question of how to tell the difference between a handmade rug and a machine-made one is often the first which the layman puts to a dealer. It is not hard to tell the difference if you know what to look for.

A hand-knotted rug has many irregularities of colour and design which add charm and individuality to a piece. A machine-made rug, by contrast, is mechanically produced and each example is a near-perfect replica of others from the same production run.

Machine-made rugs with patterns which copy well-established oriental rug designs have been made since the first quarter of the twentieth century. Some are such convincing reproductions of the originals that the layman can be confused but, with a little experience, the difference is usually quite obvious. The first clues are seen in the back and sides of the rug. Turn the rug over and examine the back. If the warp, weft and knots lie in perfect, regular and straight lines, with no variations, the rug has almost certainly been made by machine. By contrast, even the finest and most precious handmade rug will show irregularities in all these features. A further clue is that the design on most machine-made rugs will only be clear on the front while the back of the rug is usually a monochromatic canvas. On almost all hand-knotted rugs, the pattern on the back is as clearly defined as on the front.

A machine-made rug is an inexpensive, short-term floor covering; it has no investment value and is usually considerably less hard-wearing than a handmade rug.

Flat-Woven Rugs

It is thought that flat-woven rugs were made long before pile rugs. Flat-weaving is the most elementary form of rug making and wall-paintings dated to the eighth millennium BC in Catal Hüyük in central Anatolia, one of the earliest urban settlements excavated, are believed to be copies of contemporary kilims. Flat-woven rugs have served many purposes in the East; as well as their use as floor coverings, they have been employed as decorative wall hangings, curtains, bed covers and covers for many different household items. They continue to be used for the same purposes today. There

The back of a typical machine-made rug showing its rigidly straight sides and the fringes sewn on in one distinct ridge. The back is covered with perfectly straight lines and the pattern is shadowy and vague.

The back of a typical hand-knotted rug showing its irregular sides and the way the fringes are a direct continuation of the warp threads. The pattern on the back of the rug is stronger and more easily read.

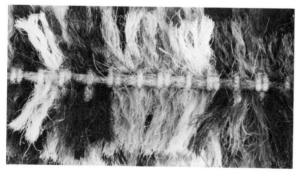 

When the pile of a machine-made rug is opened, it can be readily seen that the wool is held down by restraining threads.

In contrast, when the pile of a handmade rug is opened it is apparent that the individual pieces of wool are knotted around the warp threads.

are a number of different flat-weave techniques the most important being described below.

Kilims The Turkish word *kilim* (in Persian *gelim*) is mainly used to describe pieces made in the weft-faced plain-weave technique. This simple weaving method has been used in many parts of the world including South America, Africa, northern Europe and throughout the Orient, since prehistoric periods. The most important oriental kilims are those of Persia, Turkey and the Caucasus although kilim weaving has also been a notable folk-art in the Balkan countries to the west of Turkey (including present-day Rumania, Bulgaria, Yugoslavia, Albania and Greece) and in the south-west in Iraq and Syria.

Kilims are made by passing a weft thread in and out of the warps, after which the fabric is beaten down with a metal comb. This is basically the same technique as is used by present-day textile machines. Kilims are usually made on narrow, often portable, looms, hence they are often made in two or more separate strips which are sewn together on completion.

The pattern of the kilim is carried by the wefts and is produced by introducing different coloured weft threads. Beating down hides the warps which are usually monochrome. The colour changes which create the design are obtained by a number of different techniques. Most common is the 'slit-tapestry' technique in which the wefts are returned around the last warp of their respective colour area. Adjacent colour areas are therefore marked by a vertical slit; angled colour changes creating staggered or stepped slits.

Most, if not all, slit-tapestry woven kilims are double-sided as are kilims in which colour changes are obtained by the alternative 'single-interlocking' technique in which wefts of adjacent colour areas are tied around a shared warp. In 'double-interlocking' wefts from adjacent colour areas interlock while in 'dovetailing', a variant of the single-interlock method, a group of wefts of one colour is applied around a shared warp. The last three techniques, 'single-interlocking', 'double-interlocking' and 'dovetailing', are found mainly on Persian kilims; dovetailed colour changes are also found in some Balkan kilims.

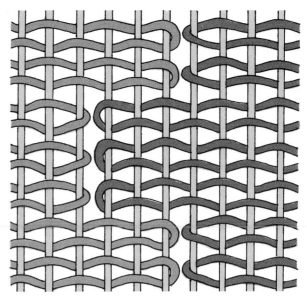

An example of the weft-faced, plain-weave technique used in kilims.

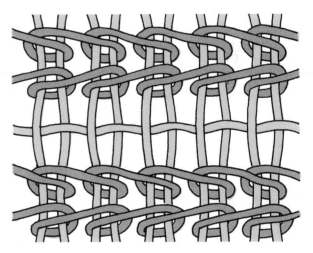

In sumak technique an additional decorative weft thread is wrapped around the warps.

Weft-wrapping or sumak-brocading The term *sumak* is traditionally used for flat-woven textiles made by the weft-wrapping technique in the Caucasus and north-west Persia. In this method, a ground weft is used to provide the foundation while coloured wefts carry the design. These wefts are normally passed over three warps and back over two warps (less often 2:1 or 4:3), forming a continuous chain structure. Sumak woven textiles are single-sided, the back showing the loose weft threads. The weft-wrapping technique was used not only for making rugs used as floor coverings, but also for wall hangings, saddle-bags, bedding bales and other domestic items.

Above: detail of a Baktiari camel bag which shows three kinds of rug-weaving technique. The centre is pile knotted, with sumak weaving at the top left and at the bottom. There is kilim work at the top right.

Opposite: a late nineteenth-century Shirvan sumak bearing a triple medallion design (10 ft 3 in×6 ft 4 in/309.6 cm×192 cm).

Other flat-weave techniques Among other flat-weave techniques used for rug making in the Orient, one of the most important is a supplementary weft-brocading method used particularly in Anatolia. Pieces produced by this technique are called *cicims* (*jijims*).

Pile-Knotted Rugs

Pile knotting is believed to be a much more recent technique than plain-weaving; there is no evidence of its use before the first millennium BC. Technically it is related to weft-wrapping, individual threads being tied by hand around the warps to form a knot. The technical details of pile-knotted rugs have already been discussed in the chapter on technical background.

The Names of Oriental Rugs

The names of oriental rugs often conjure up fascinating pictures in the mind of the rug lover — wild eastern plains with exotically robed weavers in fierce combat with the elements. In reality, the names are down-to-earth labels used to identify and classify different types of rugs. There are many systems for naming rugs and a few points of reference are: the country, area and town or village of origin, the name of the tribe or clan by which it was made, the name of the actual weaver, the market town, the name of the shape of the rug or its function and, lastly, its age.

Countries of origin The basic classification is according to the country of origin. The principal traditional rug-weaving countries (not necessarily following present-day political boundaries) are as follows:

Turkey Asiatic Turkey is also described as Anatolia or Asia Minor
Iran The name Persia is often used as a synonym for Iran, although it strictly covers a smaller area, analogous to the relationship between the Netherlands and Holland
The Caucasus This area is now part of the USSR although it is also taken to include Azerbaijan, the southern part of which is in Iran
Central Asia This is usually taken to include present-day Turkmenistan, Uzbekistan and Tadzhikistan, all now in the USSR, and also Afghanistan

East Turkestan An area which roughly corresponds to the Pamir Valley, now part of western China. Rugs from here were mainly marketed through Samarkand, and used to be called after this town
India Including present-day Pakistan
China
Egypt Important mainly for rugs made when Egypt was part of the Ottoman empire. Recently, copies of Persian rugs have been made by hand here
North Africa Including Morocco and Algeria
The Balkans Important mainly for kilims, although Rumania and Bulgaria both have hand-knotted carpet industries

Rug-weaving areas In many cases rugs are called by the name of a larger area, often corresponding to a province or geographical area, in which the rugs have been woven. In many such cases the production of the individual villages cannot, at present, be clearly distinguished. Thus, the rugs made in the villages, numbering more than one thousand, in the Hamadan area of Iran, are known as Hamadan rugs. Similarly, rugs made in the Heriz area, although possibly made in the nearby towns of Gorevan or Serab, are often classified as Heriz rugs. Other collective descriptions in Iran include north-west Persian rugs, Fars and Kirman rugs. Tientsin, Peking and Sinkiang are Chinese provinces after which rugs are named. Many Turkish rugs are called Ushak, Bergama or Konya after the geographical areas around these towns, while Shirvan and Daghestan rugs are among many examples traditionally called after old or new geographical or political areas in the Caucasus which produced rugs with individual characteristics.

Market towns Occasionally the name of the market town through which rugs were traded, was applied to rugs themselves. Thus, during the nineteenth century, a large proportion of Turkish rugs were called Smyrna rugs in the West. Another well-known example is Bokhara, the old name for Turkoman rugs in general and those made by the Tekke tribe in particular. Such names are often misleading,

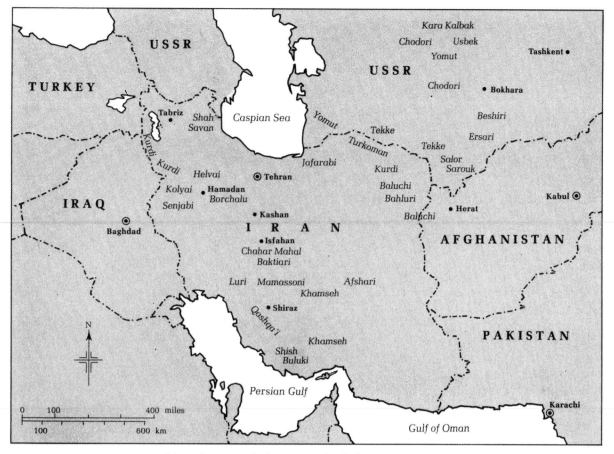

Map showing the location of tribal weavers in Iran.

since the towns after which the rugs are called sometimes produced their own, quite different rugs.

Tribal names Tribal weavings are often named after the names of the tribe and these may cross political or other territorial frontiers. For example, Kurdish rugs include rugs made in north-west Iran, eastern Anatolia and southern Iraq. Turkoman rugs originated in an area of which a part today belongs to the Soviet Union, part to northern Iran and part to Afghanistan. Baluchi rugs were and are made in eastern and south-eastern Iran, in Afghanistan and Baluchistan, and so on. Tribal names are often sub-divided, which happened when tribes or clans of one main group produced rugs with particular distinguishing features. Thus, Turkoman rugs are often named after the main known weaving tribes including the Tekke, Yomut, Salor, Saryk, Chodor, Arabatshi and Ersari, each of which produced rugs with specific designs or technical features. In the case of many other tribes, such secondary classification is more difficult since their weavings are less well documented. This applies particularly to the Yörük of eastern Anatolia and some of the tribal weavers in Iran; it is also known that some tribal names include related village weavings. An example of this is the name 'Baktiari' which is applied not only to rugs made by the tribe of that name but to those made in the villages of the Char Mahal area of Iran in which the Baktiari settled.

Individual weavers' names A minority of Persian rugs made mainly in the twentieth century, are known by the names of the master weavers to whom they are attributed. For example, Hajji Jallili was a master weaver from Tabriz; Mohtachemi was from the town of Kashan, Amogluo lived near the Holy City of Mashad. Not all the rugs made by these weavers bear a signature, but their style and workmanship is often unmistakable. Such pieces are rare and always command high prices on the international oriental rug market.

*A turn of the century Tekke rug, probably made
in the Merv area of the S.S.R. of Turkmenistan.
Its basic ornamental feature is the repeated
octagon or gul, which is Persian for 'rose'.
Much has been written about the treatment of
the gul, which varies widely from tribe to tribe.*

A late nineteenth-century Baktiari rug made to a typical garden design. Such designs were intended to represent the layout of a Persian garden and were divided into flower-beds, paths and streams with fish flowing through them. The design of garden rugs became increasingly simplified as the nineteenth century progressed. This rug should be compared with the eighteenth-century example on page 29.

Size and shape In England the word 'carpet' has traditionally been in use for larger pieces and 'rug' for smaller ones, the division between the terms sometimes being fixed as 40 square feet (approximately 4 m²). In American terminology, the word 'rug' is often used irrespective of the size of a piece, 'carpet' being reserved for wall-to-wall (fitted) carpets. For the purposes of this book, the term 'rug' will be used throughout, regardless of the shape and size of the piece in question.

In the rug trade, a number of oriental terms are used to designate rugs of specific size ranges. For example, *dozar* and *sejjade* are applied to small rugs, approximately 6 feet 6 inches by 4 feet (198 cm by 122 cm). Smaller scatter rugs, 5 feet 3 inches by 3 feet 3 inches (160 cm by 100 cm) are called *zaronim*, while other small sizes are called *namase* and *pushti* or, in English, 'baby' or 'mat'. Long, narrow rugs, commonly between 2 feet 10 inches and 3 feet 8 inches (86 cm by 112 cm) in width and varying in length from 8 feet to 30 feet (244 cm to 915 cm), are called 'runners' or *kenares*.

Function names Apart from such well-established, self-explanatory terms as prayer-rug and audience-carpet (a large prestigious rug made for royal or official receptions) many oriental terms are in use to describe specialized functional, mainly tribal, weavings. Saddle-bags (*khorjins*) are woven in many different sizes and shapes by tribal weavers over a wide area and each rug-weaving area has its own specialist vocabulary usually based on Persian or Turkish terms. The largest number of such specialized functional weavings undoubtedly belongs to the Turkoman of Central Asia and these include *ensis* (door hangings), *kapunuks* or *gapylyks* (door surrounds), *chuvals*, *torbas*, *mafrashs*, *kaps* and *jollars* (all terms for different types and sizes of tent-bags), *azmalyks* (pentagonal camel decorations), *jolami* (decorative tent-bands) and many others.

Design names Many designs have come into the rug vocabulary to describe individual types of rugs. Among examples from early rugs are the Hunting rugs (depicting animal hunting scenes) and Garden carpets (laid out in the

Above: an azmalyk, *or pentagonal camel decoration, made c.1850 by the nomadic Yomut tribe (4 ft 2 in×2 ft 11 in/127 cm×89 cm). It depicts tulips on an ivory field surrounded by a saw-edge border. At the top animals, birds and human figures form a wedding procession.*

Opposite: a festival camel decked out in necklaces, knee pads and saddle cover.

style of a formal Persian garden) from Iran, the Dragon carpets (with stylized Chinese-style dragons) from the Caucasus, and the Mille-Fleur rugs (with a field of tiny floral ornaments) made in India and copied in southern Persia. Holbein, Lotto, and Bird rugs describe specific Turkish designs, while such terms as Medallion carpet and prayer rug are more general design descriptions (the latter is a case where the name describes both the function and the design which includes a prayer-niche or *mehrab*).

Many nineteenth- and twentieth-century rugs are also known by design names. *Hatchli* describes the cross-design of many Turkoman *ensis*; Eagle- and Sunburst-Kazak is used for a design mainly used in the Karabagh area of the Caucasus and Tree of Life rug is a name given to rugs made in many different areas incorporating a naturalistic or stylized tree.

The age of a rug The age of a rug is of importance to the purchaser and, particularly with older examples, often causes controversy. Not even the basic terminology is free from disagreement. In England and other European countries, the word 'antique' is normally used to describe a rug which is more than a hundred years old. This is also the definition accepted by European customs authorities for distinguishing rugs on which no import duties are payable. In the United States, on the other hand, the term 'antique' has been traditionally used to describe articles made before the year 1800 and it is only recently that the American rug trade has tended to adopt the European use of the word.

Further sub-divisions are sometimes used by the rug trade. Thus in England the term 'semi-antique' may be applied to rugs between fifty and a hundred years old while 'old' is employed for pieces made between twenty and fifty years ago. In Germany, the same age ranges are

A mid-nineteenth-century Heriz rug (13 ft
9 in×10 ft 9 in/418.6 cm×314.6 cm) with the
centre medallion and the pale indigo spandrels
covered with stylized flowers.

Opposite: an antique Kazak (8 ft 4 in×4 ft
5 in/253 cm×132.7 cm) with a triple
Sunburst design, typical of the strong,
primitive design of the southern Caucasus.

often called 'old' and 'semi-old' respectively. Rugs which were made less than twenty years ago are classified as 'modern'.

The knowledge available about the age of a specific rug is not, however, as reliable as these trade classifications imply. With respect to many types of rugs, particularly those made more than fifty years ago, the opinions of oriental rug specialists may vary within quite wide limits. No scientific tests have been developed for determining the age of textiles which are less than about five hundred years old and with the exception of a number of types of rugs which have been dated from their appearance on old master paintings (from the fifteenth century onward) and a few rugs which have inscribed dates, most of our knowledge of the age of early rugs is based on the comparative study of designs by art historians, a method which has often led to disagreements.

It is possible to be more certain about some types of rugs made within the last hundred years, on the basis of scientific tests carried out on dyes. Particularly within the last decade, progress has been made in identifying a number of the early and later synthetic dyes which came into the oriental rug-weaving territories from about the 1860s onwards. Dye tests can therefore often establish the earliest date that a rug can have been made, although the absence of synthetic dyes cannot be considered as absolute proof of an early age; in some parts of Iran, for example, synthetic dyes did not come into general use until World War II. Much patient work which correlates the results from such dye analyses with research on the trade in dyes in the different areas, often supplemented with knowledge gained from rugs with inscribed dates, may be expected to improve our knowledge in this field in the future.

The author's translation of the dated panel on the Ardebil carpet reads as follows: 'I have no refuge in the world other than your Presence/ I have no other place to which I can turn/ The work of your loyal Servant, Maqsud Kashani, in the year 946.'

Dated Rugs

Where a date is knotted into the pile of a rug, one might assume that this would indisputably indicate its exact age. However, in a small percentage of dated rugs, this assumption is false, as an illiterate weaver may simply have copied the numerals from another rug. In other cases, a weaver's simple error of two or three knots could alter the number, and thereby date the rug a century earlier or later. To some unschooled weavers, the numbers were simply part of the design or pattern, and they did not realize the importance of carefully knotting the exact pattern devised by the artist. Examples of rugs in which the dates have been unscrupulously altered are also known.

Persian numerals are written as follows in script. Two systems are commonly found in rugs:

0	1	2	3	4	5	6	7	8	9
٠	١	٢	٣	٤	٥	٦	٧	٨	٩
٠	١	٢	٣	٤	٥	٦	٧	٨	٩

In order to read the date woven into a Persian rug, one must understand the method of converting dates from the Islamic Hegira calendar to the Christian calendar. As the Christian calendar begins with the birth of Christ, so the Islamic Hegira calendar begins with the year AD 622, when the great Prophet Mohammed took flight from Mecca, his birthplace, to Medina. The Muslim year is lunar and is therefore eleven days (or one thirty-third of a year) shorter than the Christian solar year. To convert the Islamic date, use the following simple mathematical formula:

    a Divide the woven Persian number by 33

    b Subtract the result of **a** from the woven date

    c Add 622 (the year of Mohammed's flight) to the result of **b** and this will give the Christian date

For a worked example of this method, one can take 946, the date woven into the famous Ardebil rug in the Victoria and Albert Museum, London:

    a $946 \div 33 = 28$

    b $946 - 28 = 918$

    c $918 + 622 = $ AD 1540

Part II
Care and
Maintenance

Wise selection and good maintenance are essential in helping oriental rug owners protect and enhance their investment. Always distinguishing between repairs the owner can tackle himself and those best left to experts, this section addresses itself to such practical questions as cleaning, diagnosing early signs of damage, restoration techniques and storage problems.

The first step in oriental rug repair is to match new wools and silks as closely as possible to the colours and quality of the originals.

Choosing Your Rug

Potential oriental rug owners often want to know how long a handmade rug will last. No one can give a simple answer, since the life of a rug is governed in part by the care it is given by its owner.

There is no doubt that handmade oriental rugs are extremely hard wearing – many rugs from the eighteenth century are still in use on floors today. But, only proper care will ensure that a rug will outlive its owner and be passed on to the next generation. Although rugs are primarily made and used as floor coverings, it must be remembered that they are also works of art and have an investment value. Therefore, they demand a certain amount of respect in order that they may become treasured family heirlooms.

Like any item in daily use, an oriental rug needs care and maintenance right from the start. In order to ensure the longest wear from a rug, the right type must be used in the right place, for example, a tough rug should be selected for areas which will get heavy wear and all rugs should be brushed regularly to protect the pile and foundation. All rug owners should inspect their rugs for possible damage, carrying out any restorations immediately.

The information given in this section is a guide to providing the best possible protection for rugs. The recommendations given are not hard and fast rules or regulations to be strictly adhered to; they are simply suggestions which, if followed, will extend the life of a rug.

The Uses of Handmade Rugs in East and West
Oriental rugs were first made for purely practical purposes such as floor coverings for weavers' tents, tent-bags or saddlebags for carrying possessions. Later on more decorative items were made, like tent hangings and bed covers. As man's way of life advanced, rugs began to play a more aesthetic and luxurious role; beautiful rugs were made as gifts, palaces were furnished with rugs, the decorative aspect of rugs was enhanced by the use of silk and ornate design. More recently, oriental rugs have become regarded as a form of investment, the Eastern form of stocks and shares.

As the trade routes opened between West and East, rugs slowly found their way to Western homes. They were greatly prized as floor and table coverings and as wall decorations. The later introduction of wall-to-wall machine-made carpets caused the popularity of oriental rugs to decline for a period. However, when the novelty of machine-made rugs grew stale, oriental rugs enjoyed an even greater popularity. In a world of machines, computers and sophisticated technical advancement, the unique handmade arts are sought after as an extension of individuality.

In the West today, as in the East, oriental rugs continue to fulfil both the role of a hard-wearing, practical and decorative floor, wall, bed or table covering, as well as being a secure financial investment and a hedge against inflation.

Rugs as Floor Coverings

The use of a rug of the most appropriate dimensions, age, quality and fibre in its most appropriate location will give it the optimum lifespan. During its lifetime, a rug will have to support a great deal of heavy wear and it is, therefore, important that an ideal rug be chosen for the most suitable place.

A little forethought and commonsense is all that is needed to place the right rug in the right location. Obviously, a wool-piled rug is more suitable in the kitchen than a fine silk rug. As a general guide, the heavier the wear anticipated, the heavier piled and the stronger the rug to be used – and vice versa.

The size of the rug When a rug is to be used on the floor, the size is an important factor. Oriental rugs are not made to provide a complete wall-to-wall floor covering, but are intended to be seen as a picture framed by an attractive surround of flooring. When buying an oriental rug, select one which will permit the exposure of at least a few inches, and preferably a foot or two, of flooring around it.

If a rug has been inherited and is too large to use anywhere in your home, it is advisable to exchange or part-exchange it for a more suitably sized rug. Where an oversized, inherited rug is of great sentimental value, the only way to use it on the floor is to fold part of the rug under, at the sides or ends as required. It should be noted, however, that this practice is not recommended under normal circumstances, but may be done as a last resort. Before folding the rug in this way, it should be inspected to check that the rug is not *churuk* or rotted (that the warp and weft are not dry and hard and would break with a cracking sound when folded). It is also essential that the folds be alternated at three- to four-monthly intervals (depending on the traffic flow) to ensure even wear and help prevent possible moth damage. *Never* cut the rug to fit the size of the room. This is a highly undesirable practice which not only reduces the life of the rug considerably, but also slashes its value by sometimes as much as ninety per cent.

Doormats
A doormat is the first bridge between the dirt-ridden outside world and the clean inside of a house. Dirty feet, muddy shoes and wet rubber boots will continually deposit grit, dirt and moisture on the rug. It is, therefore, important that any handmade rug to be used

as a doormat should be in good condition, with a heavy, thick and dense pile and preferably with a cotton foundation; suitable types are Sarouk, Hamadan, Baktiari and Indian rugs. It is also advisable to choose a dark-coloured rug so that the dirt will not be too obvious.

A handmade rug used as a doormat needs to be cleaned in accordance with the amount of traffic it receives, but on average every six months. The rug should be turned to change its position and allow even wear.

Rugs in Hallways
Oriental rugs are very popular in entrance halls as they provide a colourful welcome to owners and guests alike. They are also ideal for hallways, where a runner (a long narrow rug) is often used.

A ground-floor hall rug receives a considerable amount of traffic and, like oriental rugs used as doormats, the rug used should be in good condition. Experience shows that a durable rug with a cotton warp and weft, like a Hamadan, a Meshkin or an Ardebil, would last well. Ground-floor hall rugs need regular cleaning and turning to change their position. Hall runners on an upper level of a home, off bedrooms, probably receive less heavy traffic. Therefore, older, finer and more delicate rugs can be used, such as Caucasian, Kurdish or Pakistani rugs.

When using a rug in a hallway where a door may open directly on to the rug, check that the bottom of the door does not crush the pile. If such crushing occurs, either shave a little of the wood from the bottom surface of the door or move the rug to another area.

Stair Rugs
Oriental rugs are sometimes used on the stairs in the United States, but this use is not popular in Europe. Stair rugs must be carefully chosen and once in place they must be cared for. A durable runner in good condition, preferably with a cotton foundation is most suitable. Hamadan, Kirman and Mashad rugs can be used.

For the protection of the rug and your own personal safety, the runner must be properly fastened to the stairs. The best way is to secure the rug in position with metal or wooden stair rods. Never use glue, nails or tacks or sticky-

backed tape to secure an oriental rug to the stairs. Sewing the runner on to any fitted stair carpeting is also not advisable.

As the securing rod will crush the pile and because the part of the rug covering the protruding stair edge will receive the most intense wear, it is essential that the rug be moved slightly up or down the stairway every six months or so, according to the amount of wear it receives. Ideally the untrodden part of the rug which has been below the stair step should now be positioned on the stair step.

If possible, it is advisable to remove an oriental stair rug every few years and replace it with another rug from, say, the hallway. This will prevent the stair rug from receiving an excessive amount of wear in particular areas and will also give it an opportunity to straighten out.

For cleaning, a tubular vacuum cleaner or simple brush may be used while the rug is secured in position. Obviously, the rug should be removed from the staircase for major cleaning.

Living-Room Rugs
Living-rooms are used differently in different homes. Some are lived in daily as a family room, whereas others are utilized for formal entertaining only. Bearing in mind the traffic flow and the recommendations made for the varying floor surfaces (see page 61), the oriental rug choice is extensive. Popular rugs for a living-room are Kashan, Tabriz, Kirman, Isfahan, Chinese and, more recently, Indian and Rumanian rugs. A Bidjar, Heriz or Sarouk might be the choice when a lot of wear is anticipated. When lighter wear is expected, antique and silk rugs look exquisitely elegant and modern rugs, such as Pakistani rugs of Bokhara design, also look enchanting.

Oriental rugs are a very adaptable art form because they can be placed with equal success in rooms of almost any period or character, ranging from the latest contemporary design to traditional elegance. From an interior designer's point of view, one particularly valuable feature of oriental rugs is the fact they usually contain or 'pick up' almost every other colour in the room, without becoming unduly obtrusive.

Fireplace Rugs

An open fire is a most attractive and psychologically desirable source of warmth – especially in cold climates where, traditionally, the finest oriental rug in the house is placed in front of the living-room fireplace. It is here that most of the long, cold winter evenings are spent and where guests are entertained.

The positioning of a fine, oriental rug in front of a fireplace is an admirable idea except that sparks from the fire make dozens of small holes in the rug and it seems criminal for a silk or irreplaceable antique rug to be used in such a way. This national tradition cannot be changed, but neither can it be condoned.

If a handmade rug is used in front of a fireplace, it is imperative that a good fireguard be used at all times. When selecting a hearth rug, choose one with a thick pile so that, if a spark does escape from the fire, it will only singe the pile and will not burn through the foundation of the rug. The further away from the fire the rug is placed, the less it will be damaged by the heat and sparks. The intense heat around the fire will eventually dry the

In this splendid dining room two antique Saraband rugs made in western Persia, blend harmoniously with the vast expanses of oak floor and panelling.

natural oils in the wool and make the rug brittle.

As many people have a favourite chair in which they always sit by the fire, the constant wear from the chair and the friction of the foot movement will show over a long period of time. It is, therefore, necessary that any rug which is kept by a fireplace be turned around at regular intervals.

Dining-Room Rugs

As oriental rugs are so durable and resilient, they serve excellently as dining-room rugs. Whatever the dining-room rug, a certain amount of care must be taken to remove any food particles or spilt liquids at the earliest opportunity to prevent staining.

Almost any rug is suitable for a dining-room with the exception of a silk rug. Selections are usually made from Heraz, Afghan, Sarabind,

Mashad or Kirman rugs and, more recently, Pakistani, Rumanian and Indian rugs.

As a dining-room table is usually a heavy piece of furniture, it should be moved fractionally at intervals. This allows the crushed pile under the weight of the table legs to breathe again and spring back into shape. The chairs should also be moved fractionally from time to time for the same reason. It is also beneficial to a dining-room rug to replace it every four to five years with another rug in the house – the most usual one to swop it with is the living-room rug.

Study or Office Rugs

Normally, a study or office does not get continual heavy daily traffic and, therefore, a more delicate rug can be used as, of course, can sturdier rugs. Décor usually dictates which rug is chosen, but a selection can be made from Bidjar, Kashan, Isfahan, Qum, Qashqā'i or Turkish rugs. Any silk or antique rug may be used in a home study and Caucasian rugs also look extremely attractive in this setting. In the business office where the desk chair is often on castors, an added protection to the rug can be provided with the use of a thin, transparent, acrylic sheet. This is placed on top of the rug and underneath the office furniture.

As with dining-room rugs, care should be taken to move desks, filing cabinets, chairs and the perspex sheet periodically (about every six months to a year), to allow the crushed pile beneath it to breathe. If the study is used infrequently, regular inspection for moth damage to the rug should be carried out. An annual airing out-of-doors is also necessary.

Bedroom Rugs

The type of rug used in a bedroom depends on the use to which the bedroom is put, which in turn is dictated by lifestyle and tradition. Generally in Europe, the bedroom is used solely for sleeping and resting; whereas in the United States it is often used as a television room for the family as well as sleeping quarters.

If the bedroom is used for sleeping only, any rug can be used – a fine antique silk, a Savonnerie, a Pakistani rug, a kilim or even a heavy Chinese rug. Where heavier wear is anticipated, a thick-piled rug with a strong foundation should be used. Tabriz, Heriz, Kirman and,

more recently, Chinese and Indian rugs have often been the choice. The rug should, of course, be turned and the furniture resting on it moved fractionally at regular intervals.

Lastly, a note of warning: an oriental rug should never be used as a bath-mat as it absorbs and retains water. This may not only cause colour run, but also mould and mildew which will rot the warp and weft threads and ruin the rug. The same strictures apply to rugs used in the kitchen.

Floor Surfaces and Underlays

Oriental rugs can be used on any floor surface, provided it is damp free and does not have jagged edges. Surfaces in use today can be divided into three floor categories: firstly, polished wood, marble or linoleum; secondly, stone or tiled; and lastly machine-made carpeting (this is generally fitted wall-to-wall).

Polished wood, marble or linoleum surfaces

All these three surfaces are normally even and sometimes slippery. Marble and polished wood provide the most exquisite setting for the hand-made rug. Almost any type of rug can be used on any of the surfaces, but thinner piled rugs, in particular, may need an underfelt or padding to prevent slipping. The most suitable and effective underlay or padding is flat and rubberized on the lower side with compressed fibres on the upper side. The rubber grips the floor and the upper fibres hold the rug firmly in position. The rug should lie freely on top of this underlay; no nails, glue, or tape are needed to secure the rug or underlay; the rug will remain in position unaided.

When cleaning the floor, both the underlay and the rug should be removed and the area underneath should be swept clean; then both underlay and rug should be swept individually and replaced.

Stone or tiled floors When using a handmade rug on a stone or tiled floor, first check that there are no sharp or protruding edges on the surface. It is not advisable to use an oriental rug on a 'bumpy' surface, since the protruding edges would raise parts of the rug higher than the remainder of the rug and these raised areas would receive concentrated wear. In some cases, the ridges would, over a period of time,

cut into the warp and weft of the rug. An underfelt would also be required on either of these surfaces to prevent the rug from slipping.

Fitted, wall-to-wall machine-made carpeting
More and more frequently, oriental rugs are taking pride of place on top of machine-made rugs. They look and 'behave' well when properly laid. The oriental rug which does not lie flat on top of machine-made carpeting is variously described as 'wrinkling', 'creeping' or 'walking'. This has been one of the most common and frustrating problems for oriental rug owners; but it is easily overcome with the correct underfelt.

A heavy-weight oriental rug on top of a non-shag machine-made carpet does not normally move – the lighter the weight of the handmade rug and the thicker and more shaggy the pile of the machine-made carpeting, the more the oriental rug will creep. A non-creep underlay has now been introduced which is made of non-static compressed fibres which solves this problem in 95 per cent of cases. This underlay should be cut and laid in the same way as the underlay for wooden floors, and requires no additional securing either by tape, nails or by sewing.

For oriental rugs used on thin piled fitted carpets, very thin underfelt may be required; whereas with thick piled fitted carpet, a thicker and harder underfelt should be used. Ideally, when an oriental rug is to be placed on wall-to-wall carpeting, the carpeting should be plain in colour and flat piled.

Underlay Although underlay can be most beneficial in certain circumstances, it is not a necessity with every oriental rug and every floor surface. Underlay is sometimes solely a matter of personal taste where rug owners may prefer an added thickness. When underlay is used it should always be cut to a fractionally smaller size, about 1 inch smaller (2.5 cm) all around, than the rug to be laid upon it. This helps the rug lie smoothly.

A beautiful Baluchi rug, placed in the traditional position in front of an open fire, has been guarded from sparks and falling embers. The owner of this room obviously cares for rugs, as no heavy furniture has been placed on them.

Rugs as Wall Hangings

The use of the handmade oriental rug for a purely decorative and artistic purpose has been part of Eastern tradition for centuries and is enjoying increasing popularity today in the West. In palaces, museums and stately homes, for example, rugs are displayed on the wall alongside paintings by great masters – each medium harmonizing beautifully with the other. As well as their visual impact, rugs as wall hangings add a note of warmth and luxury.

Almost any rug can be used as a wall decoration provided it is not too heavy – a lighter-weight rug will not strain the warp and weft threads whereas a heavy rug will pull the threads and possibly break them. The warp and weft threads must be in good condition and must form a firm foundation.

Fine old rugs which have had heavy wear are particularly suited for use as wall hangings. An antique Kashan, for example, with little pile would last decades longer if hung on the wall rather than subjected to constant floor traffic. Other rugs, from a purely aesthetic viewpoint, are also more suited to hanging – pictorial rugs, silk rugs where the light is more beautifully reflected, and kilims. A fine silk rug such as a Qum, Isfahan or Tabriz or a silk and metal thread one, like a Hereke, Kayseri or Kashan, used as a wall hanging, is in every way as striking as any other art form – in many cases more so.

How to Hang a Rug

There are two recommended ways to hang a rug, both based on the same principle but differing according to the weight and size of the rug to be hung.

The first method is suitable for small or medium light-weight rugs no larger than 7 feet by 5 feet (213 cm by 152 cm).

● Cut a strip of fabric (heavy cotton is ideal, but never use a man-made material) or binding tape (without an adhesive backing) approximately 2 inches (5 cm) in width and to a length approximately 1 inch (2.5 cm) shorter than the width of the rug. If fabric, rather than tape, is being used, oversew all the edges to prevent fraying.

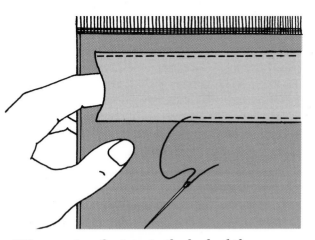

When sewing the tape to the back of the rug, ensure the pocket will be loose enough.

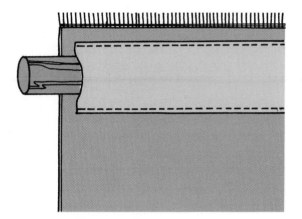

The rod should pass freely into the newly-formed pocket, or the hanging rug will pucker.

● Place the tape at the back of the rug, along the top edge about ½ inch (1.3 cm) below the line where the kilim begins and with approximately ½ inch (1.3 cm) of width to spare at either side. Check that the tape is being placed at the right end of the rug as some rugs have strictly one-way designs such as prayer rugs, Tree of Life, and The Four Seasons.
● With a strong, fine thread, oversew the tape to the back of the rug using small stitches and catching the warp and weft of the rug with every stitch. Both edges of the tape should be stitched to the rug, making a continuous sleeve. Leave the ends of the sleeve open.
● Through this newly-formed sleeve or pocket, pass a circular solid rod (wood or metal). The rod should be at least 2 inches (5 cm) longer than the width of the rug.
● Attach the support brackets to the wall, allowing just sufficient distance between the two brackets to clear the width of the rug.

64

The second method of hanging a rug should be used for large and heavy-weight rugs.

● Attach the tape to the back of the rug in the same way as for a smaller rug, but first cut the tape into 12-inch (30-cm) sections and attach the sections to the rug $\frac{1}{2}$ inch (1.3 cm) apart. These gaps permit the use of additional brackets and prevent sagging. Insert a suitable rod. Attach rod support brackets to the wall, aligned with the gaps in the tape.

● Both these methods will give the required support to the rug and will enable it to hang evenly. Attractive tassels are sometimes added to the rod at either side of the rug for further decoration.

● Periodically, the rug should be removed from the wall and placed flat on the floor for a few weeks. The spun fibres of the warp and weft, which will have been pulled for some time, will then spring back into shape and the life of the rug will be prolonged.

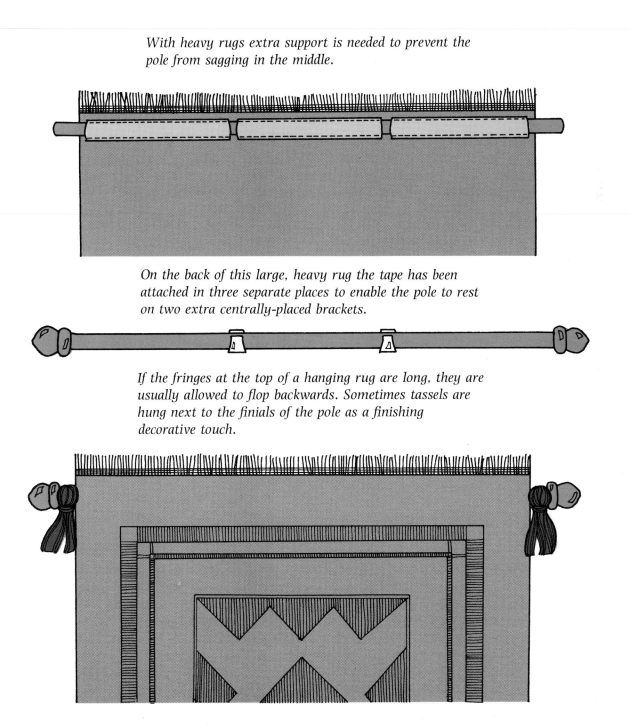

With heavy rugs extra support is needed to prevent the pole from sagging in the middle.

On the back of this large, heavy rug the tape has been attached in three separate places to enable the pole to rest on two extra centrally-placed brackets.

If the fringes at the top of a hanging rug are long, they are usually allowed to flop backwards. Sometimes tassels are hung next to the finials of the pole as a finishing decorative touch.

What Not To Do

Sewing curtain rings on to the rug is not recommended as it provides support only at the points at which the rings are attached. The use of rings over a period will produce a wave-shaped end to the rug. The use of nails, sticky tape or glue is **never** to be recommended.

With the exception of flat-woven rugs like kilims and sumaks, rugs should **not** be hung sideways on the wall for an extensive period. If this is done, the rug will become misshapen as the weft threads are more easily stretched than the warp threads. It is not advisable that heavy rugs with large woollen foundations, Afghan and Baluchi rugs come into this category, be hung for long periods of time, as the wool would stretch considerably, resulting again in a misshapen rug.

A rug should **not** be hung on a wall where it is subjected to strong, direct sunlight — this will cause general fading or, worse, fading over part of its area. Rugs should **never** be placed near or above direct heat and care should be taken to hang them away from fireplaces, air heating vents and radiators. Needless to say, a damp wall should be avoided at all costs.

Rugs as Bed and Table Coverings

Oriental rugs have been used for centuries as decorative covers for both bed and table and this very Eastern tradition continues in the West, particularly in Belgium, Holland, West Germany and other northern countries where rugs are sometimes seen as furniture coverings.

The flat-weave kilim rugs, due to their pliable texture and light weight, make excellent decorative pieces for such purposes, as well as small antique rugs with a thinner pile. As rugs used for decorating tables and beds are not abused by soiled foot traffic, even the most rare antique silk masterpiece may be used. On the other hand, a small Pakistani rug can be just as alluring and effective.

Whenever a rug is used as a tablecloth or cover, it must be remembered that any heavy ornament placed upon it should be moved fractionally on a regular basis to allow the pile to breathe and avoid being crushed. One should also beware of leakage from floral arrangements and potted plants placed upon the rug, as this moisture will rot the rug foundation.

Although some Orientals sit cross-legged upon their rugs at mealtimes and a feast of dishes is placed before them, the adaptation of this tradition is not recommended for Westerners. Resilient as rugs are, the inevitable deposits of grease, food particles and liquids etc are not conducive to rug cleanliness or longevity. Always, therefore, remove your rug from the table before dining.

A fine, antique silk Hereke prayer rug appropriately hung so that it glows like a jewel. The clock, however, has been damagingly placed on the Kashan rug beneath.

Daily Care and Cleaning

The day-to-day care of an oriental rug is no more complicated than looking after any other household furnishing. Most home items carry a label giving a few recommendations as to the care that should be given to them – unfortunately, this is rarely the case with oriental rugs and in this section, the general guidelines for everyday care are given.

Cleanliness is perhaps the most important factor concerning the long-term preservation of any rug. As shall be seen further on in the book, dirt – if unlodged and ground into the rug's foundation – can cause untold damage. Cleaning a rug makes it look good and it also prolongs its life.

For daily removal of surface particles of dirt and dust, a good hand broom should be used. It is also essential that the rug be moved and the underlying area swept clean. A non-electric hand carpet sweeper may also be used for this purpose.

Any earnest rug preserver would not favour the daily use of a powerful, electric vacuum cleaner (although one can appreciate the time-saving service it renders) which can pull the knots out of the rug with its strong air suction. With today's frenetic pace of life, I concede to the use of a vacuum cleaner about once a month, provided it is not too powerful and does not have rotary brushes. A low-powered vacuum cleaner with a nozzle attachment can be most effective when used on stair rugs.

A warning to vacuum-cleaner users: only vacuum the pile of the rug, not the delicate fringes. The fringes will not last long if a vacuum cleaner is used on them regularly.

Use of the vacuum cleaner, with a built-in 'beater', on the back of the rug every six months is an excellent idea for removing ground-in loose fibres, sand, dirt and grit.

With the increasing importance, value and scarcity of handmade rugs today, there is only one method of cleaning that I can recommend without reservation: hand cleaning. Quite simply, a rug made by hand needs to be cleaned by hand. No two rugs are exactly alike and each rug requires individual treatment. Even within a single rug different areas need different care, depending on the amount of wear and tear to which they are subjected. Such individual attention is only possible with careful hand cleaning and can never be given by a machine.

Cleaning a rug by hand is a time-consuming process and, when carried out by an expert, will be more expensive than machine cleaning. Therefore, as a second and cheaper choice, a rug may be taken to professional, specialized oriental rug-cleaning companies (not to be confused with companies cleaning machine-made carpeting) which have years of experience and most sophisticated machinery, especially designed for the cleaning of handmade rugs. I must stress however, that no old, antique or silk handmade rugs should be cleaned by machine under any circumstances.

Cleanliness is probably the best defence against any damage. Regular cleaning, of course, protects the investment value of the rug; the money spent on cleaning is fractional, compared to the rug's constantly appreciating value.

How to know when a rug needs cleaning An expert's advice is not normally required to determine when a rug needs cleaning. A rug with a light background and open field cries out for cleaning when dirty. However, with a rug of a darker hue and with a more intricate pattern, it is a little less obvious. The first sign will be the feel of the pile, which will be somewhat matted and rough – not soft and velvety as it should be. You can also see the dirt by folding one corner of the rug; and with the cupped palm of the hand under the pile, tap the back of the rug with the other hand. If grit, broken wool fibres or dust, sprinkle into the palm of your hand, it is time for cleaning. This test is both important and accurate.

How often cleaning is required varies from rug to rug, home to home, family to family and is dependent on the owner's lifestyle. As a very general guide, I recommend that rugs in daily use on the floor be cleaned at least every two years.

Hand Cleaning at Home

The idea of attempting to hand clean an oriental rug at home may seem daunting, yet it can be carried out successfully by the amateur at virtually no cost. Provided the simple step-by-step instructions are followed, the results will amaze even the most dubious.

The great majority of rugs can be hand cleaned by the layman, but rugs in the following categories should not be attempted by a non-expert: antique rugs; silk or part silk rugs, whether antique, old or contemporary, and seriously damaged rugs in need of major restoration. The rugs in these three groups are normally extremely delicate and may be most valuable; only experienced hands can assure successful cleaning. The slightest error by the unpractised could result in costly and irreparable damage. If there is any doubt as to whether a rug can be cleaned at home, consult your local dealer. He will gladly advise you as to whether the cleaning can be done at home, if he can do it for you, or refer you to another professional who specializes in such cleaning.

Preparation for hand cleaning The preparation for hand cleaning is as important as the hand cleaning itself. For comfort, small rugs can be cleaned on a raised surface, like a table. The following steps should be taken prior to cleaning:

The rug should be inspected for possible damage which may need repair. If damage is found, this area should be sewn together temporarily to prevent the damage going further and immediately attended to after cleaning.

Turning the corner of a rug pile-downwards on the palm of the hand to test it for dirt.

If after tapping the back of the rug, dirt falls into the palm, the rug needs cleaning.

Repairs which require repiling should be carried out after cleaning in order to best match the wools.

All dirt, dust, grit, sand, broken fibres, and other extraneous material, must be removed from the rug. Gentle beating on the back of the rug with a traditional cane beater is the best way to leave the rug dirt free. Make sure that this is carried out thoroughly and that no particles remain; otherwise, when wetted during the hand-cleaning process, such particles will turn to a mud-like substance which, when dried, will act as an abrasive cement. Taking short cuts when removing this dirt will leave the pile of the rug rough and shaggy after cleaning; and it will also eventually reduce the life of the rug.

Any specific stain on the rug should be removed prior to cleaning. If these are not properly treated beforehand, the hand-cleaning process will cause the stain to 'set' and it will be more difficult, and sometimes even impossible, to remove this at a later stage.

A colour fastness test should be done before cleaning is started. This can be done by test cleaning a small highly-patterned area of the rug. Wipe this area with a damp white cloth or towel. Provided no colour penetrates the cloth, the rug is colour fast. If the colour bleeds on to the cloth, the rug should not be cleaned at home, but given to a professional.

Equipment needed for hand cleaning Hand cleaning requires considerable time, effort and patience; the equipment needed is minimal by comparison. Most items will probably already be in the house: a bucket, brush, vinegar and carpet shampoo.

The brush that assures most successful results is a fine horse brush used for grooming. These are available in varying sizes and fibres; select one with soft bristles of an approximate depth of 1 inch (2.5 cm). The bristles should be made from a natural fibre, not plastic or any other man-made fibre.

The most suitable type of rug shampoo to use is one that will dry to a powder after it has been applied to the rug. The suspended dried soil and solution can then be removed by vacuum cleaner or brush.

To mix the solution for cleaning, use the proportions of half a cup of rug shampoo to

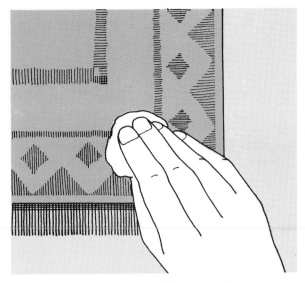

Before beginning the hand cleaning of a rug, it is essential to first test for colour-fastness using a white cotton cloth.

If any dye comes off on the white cloth, the rug should be cleaned by an expert as there is likely to be a colour-run problem.

Opposite: a patina of dirt and grime will naturally develop on an oriental rug over the years and it is not immediately noticeable to the owner who sees the rug every day. This dramatic photograph, in which a rug has been half-cleaned, shows how a veil of dirt can be lifted to reveal glowing colours and designs the owner may have forgotten.

No complicated equipment is needed for hand cleaning an oriental rug. Such materials as these can be found in almost every household.

four and a half cups of warm water (never use hot or boiling water). One tablespoon of white (natural) vinegar should then be added. This prevents any possible colour run, and helps bring out the natural lustre of the wool.

How to Clean
With a dirt-free rug and mixed cleaning solution ready, surface cleaning can be carefully carried out as follows:

● Lay the rug on a flat, hard surface (if the size permits then use a table) with the pile of the rug facing upwards. Dip the brush into the prepared solution and starting at one corner of the rug, begin to dispense the solution by gently massaging it into the pile. Brush in a gentle up and down movement, with and against the pile. Hard rubbing or brushing will not clean the rug more thoroughly and may even damage it. The amount of solution and

brush pressure should be as constant and even as possible. Avoid soaking the rug, as over-wetting can damage the foundation. Progress across the pile of the rug with short, over-lapping movements until the entire surface is cleaned. End with a brushing movement in the direction of the pile. The fringes do not normally require cleaning but they may be brushed carefully with solution if necessary. Here again, do not soak them and ensure that a very gentle motion is used.
● During cleaning, handle the rug with added care as it is more delicate than usual in its damp condition; the chances of potential damage are therefore increased.
● It is neither necessary nor advisable to wet clean the back of the rug, for it does not come into direct contact with dirt. Carefully, remove the rug for drying — try not to fold it while wetted, but carry it flat or rolled. Weather permitting, lay the rug outside to dry in natural sunlight on a clothes line (only light-weight and small rugs can be hung on a clothes line) or on a hard and dry surface. It is not advisable to dry the rug on a lawn as the rug would

further absorb and retain the moisture of the grass. If climatic conditions provide no warm sun, the alternative is to dry the rug flat at home, preferably where there is a warm air current heating system. Placing a damp rug back on the floor will damage its foundation and, over a period of time, will cause disintegration of the rug; therefore, check that it is completely dry before doing so. The warp, weft and pile of a fully dried rug should feel soft and pliable.

● Remove the dried dirt and shampoo powder from the rug by brushing or gently vacuum-ing. Clean and rinse the brush thoroughly with warm water and leave to dry.

Hand cleaning has multiple rewards for the patient individual who tackles the job himself: great personal satisfaction, the distinctly improved appearance of the rug and the knowledge that the rug has been given a new lease of life. Yet, perhaps most rewarding of all is the greater affinity and understanding that develops through this cleaning – every tiny motif, every subtlety of shade and every nuance previously unseen by the owner, has now come into view.

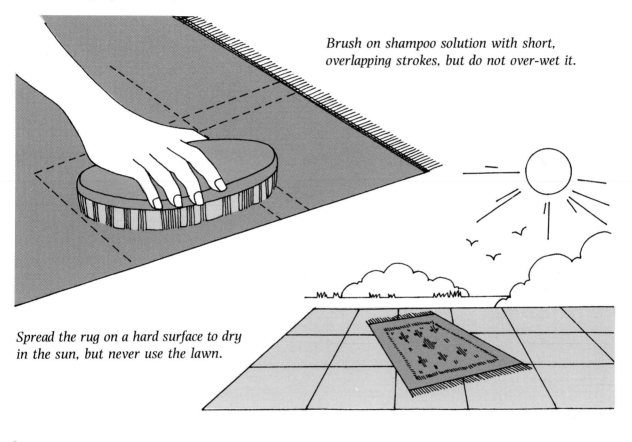

Brush on shampoo solution with short, overlapping strokes, but do not over-wet it.

Spread the rug on a hard surface to dry in the sun, but never use the lawn.

After the rug is dry, gently brush it in the direction of the pile to remove dried shampoo.

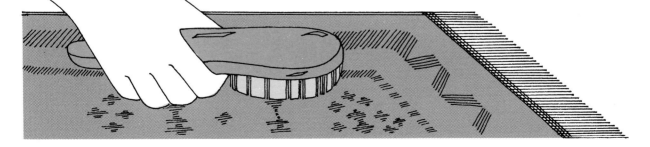

What Not To Do

As a further plea for rug preservation, the following unacceptable ways of cleaning handmade rugs are mentioned. Some readers may be mildly amused by this list but many destructive results have been wrought on helpless rugs subjected to these unfortunate actions.

Washing machines A washing machine is for the cleaning of clothing, and should not be used for irreplaceable works of art. Obviously, the detergent, water temperature and vibrations can leave a rug with cement-like wool, no lustre, colour run and the entire rug may even end up in shreds.

Dry-cleaning Dry-cleaners often advertise their expertise as rug cleaners, but this is limited to the handling of machine-made rugs and not to hand-knotted masterpieces. Some cleaning solutions used by dry-cleaners ruin the wool and damage the warp and weft. Such damage is irreparable, not even a rug weaver or restorer can rectify this. Sometimes, the full damage done by dry-cleaning is not seen for a matter of months and, if no guarantee is given at the time of cleaning, then there can be no redress.

Water soaking The complete immersion of a rug in a bath of water or the hosing down of a rug has sometimes been recommended. This is not advisable for, in most cases, especially with modern rugs, it can cause colour run. In addition, the warp and weft threads are soaked unnecessarily, for they do not need cleaning, as they are less exposed to dirt, being completely encased by the single fibres which form the knots. Such soaking of the foundation can cause damage when not fully dried.

In some books and films, there are scenes of Persians soaking and washing rugs in rivers and, therefore, many people wrongly believe that this cleaning method is correct. It is important to note that only rugs of recent manufacture (never antique or silk rugs) are subjected to this process. This soaking and washing is carried out to remove the millions of wool fibres embedded in the pile after the rug has been trimmed and cut down from the loom. The water is cold, the process is carried out in a very short time and the rug is immediately laid out in the hot sun to dry completely.

Powered rotary-brush cleaners These machines are often available for rent; they were invented specifically to clean machine-made carpeting and not fine, handmade floor coverings. The heavy, circular brushes have coarse bristles which, when powered in a circular motion, will twist and break the fibres of the pile of an oriental rug.

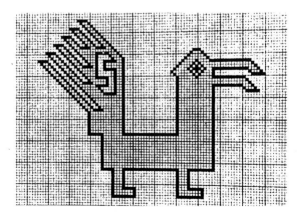

To get rid of loose dirt, turn a rug pile-downwards, before lifting a corner and beating it gently on the back using a flexible light-weight cane beater.

Beating The periodic beating or shaking of a rug outdoors is recommended. The amount of wear it receives dictates how often this should be done. An old-fashioned carpet beater is the best implement for this. Small and finely knotted rugs should be hung outside on a clothes line and should be beaten gently on the back. Heavy and larger rugs should be placed pile downwards on a dry floor. You then hold one corner, elevate part of the rug and beat it softly. It is vital that this beating should not be done too harshly. This beating action should always be applied to the back of the rug, allowing all the dirt to fall to the ground from both the back and front of the rug.

Antique and silk rugs should not be cleaned in this way; they require professional attention to assure their preservation.

Turning The term 'turning' means turning the rug around one hundred and eighty degrees to change its position; thus ensuring even wear all over the rug. The turning of a rug is a protective measure and all rugs need to be turned regularly during their use on the floor. The heavier the traffic, the more often the rug should be turned. Oriental rugs in an entrance hall and those used as doormats obviously need more regular turning than bedroom or study rugs. From time to time, it is advisable to replace rugs which have been subjected to a lot of tread with others which have had lighter wear.

Heavy furniture Where possible, avoid placing heavy furniture on oriental rugs for long periods of time. The weight of such items crushes the pile and can damage the rug's foundation. The placing of furniture cups (similar to small ashtrays) under the furniture legs helps disperse the pressure from a concentrated area and also prevents sharp furniture edges from damaging the rug. Every few months, the furniture should be moved slightly (lift the furniture to move it; do not drag it across the rug) to allow the crushed pile to breathe. When the furniture is moved, the pile of the area on which the furniture rested may be matted together. To rectify this, dampen the matted area and gently play with the wool with your fingers until the pile springs back into shape.

Placing furniture on an oriental rug is often unavoidable. To diffuse the weight of furniture and reduce possible damage to the rug, wooden or plastic cups should be placed under the feet of heavy or sharp pieces.

Moths Damage from moth larvae should not occur if a rug is properly cleaned and turned. Moths favour undisturbed areas such as: underneath grandfather clocks, under beds and undisturbed areas on which a rug may lie. Regular cleaning is therefore essential.

An added protection from moths can be provided by airing a rug out-of-doors, turning both the back and the front of the rug to the natural sunlight. The rug should be laid flat on a dry surface for some hours.

Damp Dampness is the enemy of an oriental rug and care must be taken to ensure that rugs are not used or stored in damp areas. Moisture is easily absorbed by the rug and will eventually rot the foundation and make the rug brittle. Dampened dirt in a rug is also dangerous as, like glue, when dried it forms splinters that cut the knots and foundations. As it is impossible to repair a damp-rotted rug, it is absolutely essential to prevent the rot in the first place.

Intense heat Any form of direct or intense heat — heat from an open fire, heat from a radiator, and the worst, that from heated flooring, is damaging to handmade rugs. Such high-level heat dries the natural oils in the wool, making it brittle and lustreless. Care should be taken to avoid placing rugs in these undesirable conditions.

Direct sunlight Rugs should be used and kept in light areas to avoid possible moth damage, but strong, direct sunlight over a long period will fade the colours. This is yet another important reason for turning the rug periodically, thus ensuring that any fading will occur all over and not just at one end or corner of the rug.

Domestic animals Most animals seem to love oriental rugs. Untrained animals or animals that are not properly exercised create a problem. They will often select a leg of furniture or a rug as their urinating spot and will return to the same spot time and time again. The acid in the urine can severely affect the colouring of the rug. Continual urination will eventually rot the rug altogether. Any urine must be cleaned up immediately. If the urine is left unattended for some time, it is almost impossible to remove at a later stage. It is, therefore, best to keep untrained pets away from rugs.

Bumps and wrinkles Bumps and wrinkles in an oriental rug occur most frequently in rugs where the foundation is of wool, as in Afghan, Kurdish and certain modern Pakistani rugs. The woollen fibre of the warp and of the weft stretches and pulls with use and does not contract again. Wrinkling may also be the result of the use of unevenly spun warp or weft thread fibres; mishandling by folding a rug for transporting; or possibly continuous traffic on one side or part of a rug which has been used without underfelt.

Unfortunately, there is very little that can be done to rectify the wrinkling in oriental rugs. Where the bump is minor, a professional rug restorer can insert new foundation threads if the old ones have been stretched or damaged. If the damage is more extensive, the specialist may have to remove the wrinkled section of the rug and resew it in order to enable it to lie flat.

When the first sign of a bump or wrinkle is noticed, the most effective home remedy is to remove the rug to an area where it will be trodden on much less. This will not cure the problem, but it will certainly prevent the bump becoming more acute.

Dealing with Accidents

*W*ater damage is perhaps the greatest enemy of the oriental rug. It can happen in many ways: flooding, leaking roofs, burst pipes, leaking radiators or simply a bucket knocked over. As with all damage to rugs, the essence of successful treatment is speed. As soon as water damage occurs, the following steps must be taken immediately:

● Absorb all the excess water from the wet area of the rug. This should be done with an absorbent towel, sponge, tissue or cloth made from an undyed cotton. The material should be placed above and below the rug and a mopping motion used. Ensure that all the water is removed.

● Sponge the damaged area with clean water, but do not soak. On no account should any carpet shampoo be used.

● Dry the wetted area immediately with warm air – a hair-dryer with variable temperature settings is probably best for this purpose. (Make sure to dry the back and front of the rug.) Do not set the temperature at the highest setting; a warm current is sufficient. The wetted area must be completely dried. Whether or not the rug is completely dried can be ascertained from its feel and texture; if it feels more leathery and harder than the rest of the undamaged area of the rug, then it is not yet fully dry.

● After the drying process has been completed the wool fibres may be matted together. This can be rectified by separating the fibres with a rubbing movement of the fingers.

Failure to carry out the above steps at the earliest opportunity may cause the warp and

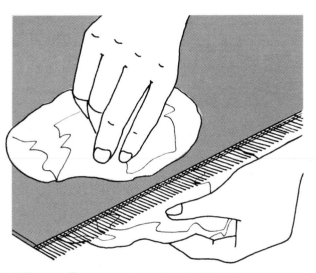

When spills occur, immediately blot the affected area from two sides.

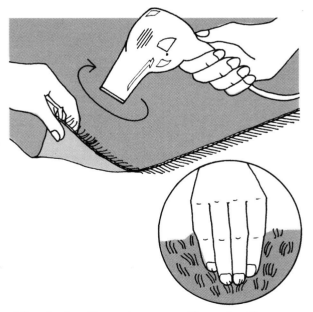

After drying the wet area, gently revive the nap of the rug with the fingers.

weft to rot. As they gradually dry the damaged area will become brittle and perished. It may also result in colour run; if this has occurred, and the degree of unsightliness merits the action, the rug will need the attention of an expert restorer either to bleach out the offending colour or, more often, to delicately repile parts of the damaged area. It is not recommended that the layman tackle a colour run problem. Such well-meaning but inexperienced handling could make the damage even more acute.

Stain Removal

Spillage and stains are inevitable in busy households, particularly ones in which there are children and pets. Provided swift and correct action is taken, spillage need not affect oriental rugs. Most spills can be removed by following the instructions below, and the items needed for carrying out the stain removing job successfully are usually everyday household items. These stain removal methods are not necessarily the same as those used by professional spot removers, but the results can be just as good, provided action is taken immediately.

There may be instances not covered in this section which will require the services of a professional. A case in point is the removal of stains on valuable antique and silk rugs which should not be attempted at home – expert attention is absolutely necessary here.

When any substance or liquid is spilt on an oriental rug, the spill should be absorbed immediately by blotting the area with uncoloured paper towels or any natural unstarched piece of cloth. This simple absorption process, when carried out at the very soonest, is the greatest contribution to successful stain removal; the longer the spill remains on the rug, the more difficult it is to remove.

Before any of the following stain removal methods are carried out, a colour fastness test should be done to ensure that the colour of the fibre will not run or bleed.

First Steps in Stain Removal

Test for fastness by wiping a small, colourful area of the rug with a damp white cloth or handkerchief. If the colour is fast, the stain may be removed at home. If it is not fast, an expert will have to do the job. Even when the colour is not fast, the spillage should still be blotted up as this will help the expert when he comes to removing the stain.

When the spillage has been absorbed and the colour-fast test has proved positive, the stain may be removed at home. When working with a stained area, start at one end of the stain and work upwards or downwards; it is inadvisable to start at the centre and work outwards as this may make the staining more extensive. Neither is it advisable to rub or brush the spot more than is necessary.

The thorough drying of the stained area after the stain has been removed is essential before the rug is put back into use. If weather conditions preclude natural drying in the sun, a hair-dryer may be used to dry the area, provided the temperature is set as low as possible.

There are a variety of stains which may affect oriental rugs and the treatment for different types varies, as can be seen from the chart in the following pages.

Urine stains are particularly common and can be most damaging to oriental rugs if left unattended. There will be no serious damage if the urine is absorbed immediately; but if it is left to dry, it is almost impossible to remove and will leave a stubborn and unsightly stain. Urine affects the rug fibres chemically and bleaches the wool as well as rotting the foundation. A particular problem with dried animal urine is that the animal will often return to the same spot to urinate time and time again, thus making the situation even more serious.

In the case of stains caused by tea, coffee, soft drinks, juices, milk, ice cream or alcohol never use soap or carpet shampoo as this will make them even more stubborn. With stains caused by blood, egg or wet gelatine, never use hot water as this will set them.

In the average family, pets have the run of the house and it is not practical to keep them away from oriental rugs. Urine stains from young, untrained animals should be dealt with immediately. Although unsightly, moulted animal hair is not harmful to oriental rugs, but should be removed by hand brushing or with a vacuum nozzle. Heavy, upright vacuum cleaners should never be used.

Stain removal chart

Urine

1 Absorb excess moisture with an undyed piece of material. Sponge the area with clean, lukewarm water. Repeat this sequence several times

2 Mix 2 tablespoons of white vinegar with 1 pint (0.5 litre) lukewarm water and work into the affected area. After a few minutes rinse with a sponge soaked in clean, warm water. Repeat if required

3 Blot dry by placing layers of white blotting paper or undyed, unstarched cotton material, under and on top of the wet area. Weight down with heavy books

Tea, Coffee, Soft Drinks, Juices, Milk, Ice Cream, Alcohol

1 Absorb the excess moisture. Sponge the area thoroughly with clean, lukewarm water

2 Mix 1 tablespoon of detergent* with 1 pint (0.5 litre) of lukewarm water and apply to the area. Repeat if necessary

3 To dry – blot area with an undyed cloth or blow dry with a hair-dryer set on the lowest setting

Cocoa, Chocolate, Gravy, Shoe Polish

1 Absorb excess moisture. Sponge the spot with clean, lukewarm water, removing as much of the spillage as possible

2 Mix 1 cup of soapless carpet shampoo or detergent to 4 cups of lukewarm water and rub affected area

3 Rinse well with clean, lukewarm water. Blot area to dry it thoroughly

*The use of non-alkaline detergents is recommended throughout.

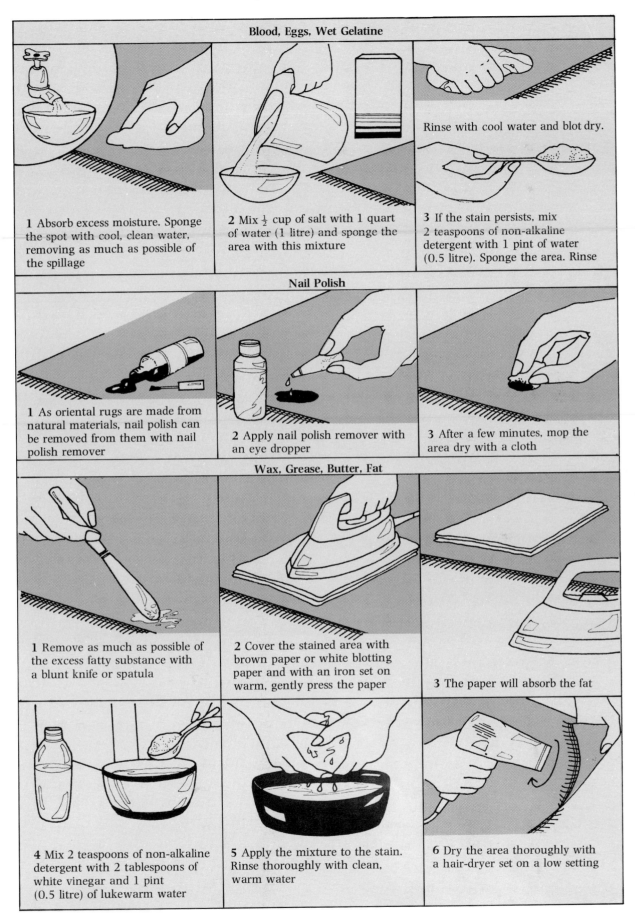

Blood, Eggs, Wet Gelatine

1 Absorb excess moisture. Sponge the spot with cool, clean water, removing as much as possible of the spillage

2 Mix ½ cup of salt with 1 quart of water (1 litre) and sponge the area with this mixture

Rinse with cool water and blot dry.

3 If the stain persists, mix 2 teaspoons of non-alkaline detergent with 1 pint of water (0.5 litre). Sponge the area. Rinse

Nail Polish

1 As oriental rugs are made from natural materials, nail polish can be removed from them with nail polish remover

2 Apply nail polish remover with an eye dropper

3 After a few minutes, mop the area dry with a cloth

Wax, Grease, Butter, Fat

1 Remove as much as possible of the excess fatty substance with a blunt knife or spatula

2 Cover the stained area with brown paper or white blotting paper and with an iron set on warm, gently press the paper

3 The paper will absorb the fat

4 Mix 2 teaspoons of non-alkaline detergent with 2 tablespoons of white vinegar and 1 pint (0.5 litre) of lukewarm water

5 Apply the mixture to the stain. Rinse thoroughly with clean, warm water

6 Dry the area thoroughly with a hair-dryer set on a low setting

Repairs and Restoration

Essential tools and materials for repairing and restoring oriental rugs can usually be found in most homes. These materials and some of the tools are the same as those originally used for weaving rugs in the Orient.

Obviously the materials that can be found in the West are not exactly the same colour or quality as the ones used when the rug was woven; but it is important to try and match these materials as closely as possible to the original ones. All the materials such as wool, goat-hair or cotton used for the foundation and the wool and silk for piling, should be pure, natural fibres and not a mixture of man-made and natural fibres.

Sewing threads are vital to restoring and should be of pure cotton. To facilitate sewing through the knots of rugs, the cotton should first be treated with beeswax. To wax a thread

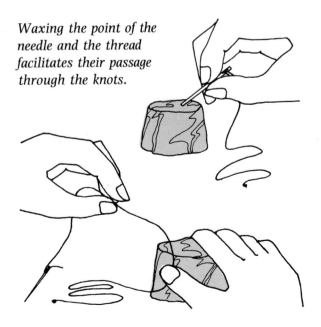

Waxing the point of the needle and the thread facilitates their passage through the knots.

simply pull it over a lump of beeswax. To help the needle pass through the knots of the rug, its point should be waxed by pushing it slightly into the wax each time.

The tools used by professional rug restorers are almost the same as the ones used for rug weaving, such as specially shaped handmade scissors, hooks and a special metal comb. A professional rug restorer needs different kinds and sizes of hooks for reweaving and repiling different rugs, and also small combs for reweaving small areas.

For the layman, it is suggested that needles should be used when repiling instead of hooks. The basic tools required for restoration are: a pair of curved (nail) scissors, a pair of dressmaking scissors, beeswax, a thimble, suitable sized needles and a small pair of pliers which are needed for pulling or pushing the needle in and out while repairing stiff rugs. A special heavy, metal comb is used by professional restorers for beating down the fabric, but this is not vital. If necessary, a fork could be used.

Major and Minor Repairs

Before attempting to carry out any of the repairs discussed in this section at home, it is essential to differentiate between minor and major repairs; for the latter professional care is needed. If a rug seems seriously damaged, it should be taken to a dealer for advice; he will either arrange for your rug to be restored by his own professional restorer or perhaps he may recommend where and how to have the rug restored. On the other hand, he may not recommend that repair work be carried out at all. Restoration may be too costly in propor-

tion to the value of the rug, or the damage may be so serious that restoration, even by an expert craftsman, may be impossible. But, even if a rug looks completely threadbare, *do not throw it away as it might be valuable* — but only an expert can tell.

It is not advisable to carry out repair work at home on valuable rugs, especially antique and silk ones. Such delicate rugs need careful handling and even a small error in mending them could prove fatal. If there is any doubt as to whether a repair should be attempted at home, then an expert opinion should be sought.

There is one instance in which repair work cannot be undertaken on a rug and that is when the rug is *churuk*. The term *churuk* means that the foundations of the rug have become damaged or rotted. A rug which is *churuk* will be brittle when folded and will give off a sound

The professional rug repairer uses special hooks and a comb which are not available in the West. For laymen attempting repairs, the materials can be found in any needlework basket.

like the cracking of finger joints.

There are two main causes of *churuk*; the first is damp, which rots the foundation of the rug, and the second is dirt which has not been cleaned off the rug. This dirt will gradually work its way through the gaps between the knots and the foundations and will in time cause the rug to lose its pliability. Unfortunately, there is nothing that can be done once *churuk* has set in and most rugs will depreciate in value as a result of it. *Churuk* rugs should be used in areas where they will get little tread and should not be hung or folded.

The fringes

Most rugs begin and end with a fringe and, during a rug's lifetime on the floor, it is inevitable that damage to these fringes will occur. Although a good-looking fringe is an attractive feature of a rug, its true function is to protect the pile. A damaged fringe endangers the knots, which make up the fabric of the rug, and these will start to disappear without the fringe as a 'guard'.

Many people, particularly Americans, prefer a long fringe on an oriental rug. This, perhaps, makes for a better-looking rug from the decorative standpoint but, from the point of view of preserving the rug, it is impractical for a num-

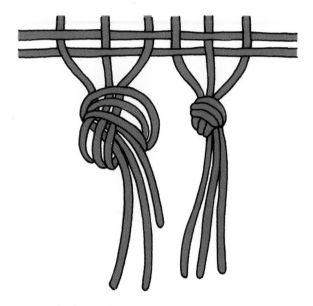

A simple fringe knot to secure the wefts.

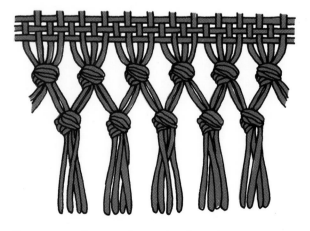

Stronger and more decorative knotting.

ber of reasons. Firstly, constant traffic on a long fringe stretches the fibres and these will eventually break, often at the point where the pile begins. Secondly, the threads of a long fringe become matted or knotted together and frequently cause accidents especially when high-heeled shoes get caught in them. Thirdly, animals, especially cats with sharp claws, find a long fringe an excellent toy and tend to pull it out.

The maximum desirable length for a fringe is approximately 1½ inches (3.8 cm) – this is both an attractive as well as a protective length. If the fringe of the rug is shorter than 1½ inches (3.8 cm), it is of no consequence and should be left as it is. If, on the other hand, it is longer, it should be trimmed to this recommended length.

To trim the fringe, the rug should be placed on an elevated flat surface, a table or a desk would be suitable, with the fringe hanging freely. Hold the fringe threads between two fingers and cut the threads, above your fingers, evenly to approximately 1½ inches (3.8 cm) in length with a sharp pair of scissors (see diagram).

There are rugs which begin and some which end with a woven section of kilim work and some which have no fringe at all; some Sarouks, Kurdish rugs and Hamadans fall into this category. This kilim work at the ends of the rug is characteristic of certain rugs and should not be removed or tampered with.

Some rugs may have a knotted fringe; such knots are adjacent to the rows of kilim work at the ends of the rug. These knots are to prevent the kilim end from fraying and should not be untied. If certain knots have worked loose, these can be retied by taking the same number of single fringe threads as used for the remaining knots (usually between two and six threads), and simply knotting them together. The knot should be as close to the kilim end as possible. The fewer fringe threads taken to make one knot, the finer and smaller the knot and the better the protection provided. More ornate knots can also be made and one of these is illustrated.

On a rug with woollen fringes it is not recommended to add too many knots. This is because the knots are susceptible to heavy wear and cause the fringes to disintegrate.

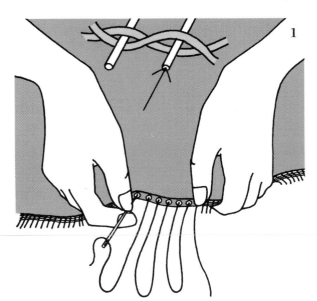

Sewing a warp thread into the first eye.

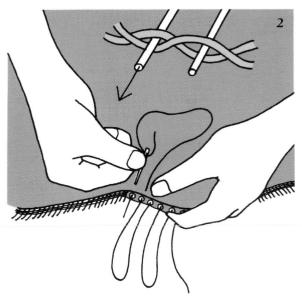

Returning the needle through the second eye.

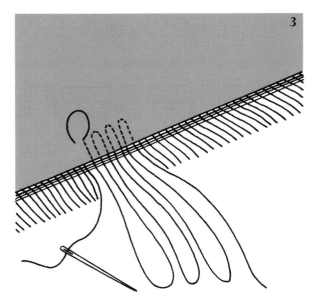

Completing the re-insertion of missing fringes.

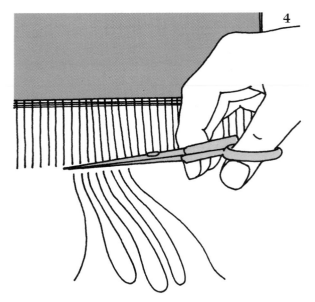

Trimming the new fringes to length.

Repairing Partly Damaged Fringes

When there are only a few fringes missing or damaged, this can easily be attended to at home. This repair is one which almost every rug owner can confidently tackle. It involves the sewing of new fringe threads as follows:

● Select thread which is the same colour and fibre as the remainder of the fringe, for example, white cotton or brown wool, and a medium-sized needle with an adequate eye.

● Place the rug on a flat surface, pile downwards and the back of the rug facing upwards.

● Leaving at least the same length of thread as the remaining fringe, align the needle to pass through the first broken warp thread (the fringe being an unpiled extension of the warp threads which form the foundation of the rug). Insert the needle through the knot to at least $\frac{1}{2}$ inch (1.3 cm) depth. Returning the needle parallel to the first stitch, pass it through the second warp thread around which the same knot is tied. Leaving at least two fringe lengths of new thread loose, continue to resew the new fringe in this manner.

● On completion, cut the looped threads and trim them evenly to the same length as the old fringe.

85

Repairing Completely Damaged Fringes

When the fringe of a rug is completely damaged or is entirely missing, speedy attention is needed to prevent the disintegration of the pile. There are two ways to approach this problem. Either a new fringe can be resewn into the rug, or a machine-made fringe, a 'false' fringe, can be added.

Resewing the fringe is the better of the two methods as this reinstates the value of the rug, restoring it to its original form. This process can be carried out in the same way as repairing partly damaged or missing fringes, provided that the last row of knots where the fringe has broken remain in position and are undamaged. If the rug is comparatively coarsely knotted, resewing a complete new fringe can be done successfully by the layman. Although it is a time-consuming job requiring patience, the results are excellent and rewarding. Antique,

silk and finely knotted rugs, and especially rugs with brittle, damaged or missing knots, should be left to the experts.

Machine-made Fringes

If it is not possible to sew a new fringe on to the rug, the alternative is to sew machine-made fringing to the ends of the rug. To most collectors and enthusiasts, machine-made fringing is undesirable, being regarded as incompatible with the original work. However, practically speaking, it serves a protective purpose and I would rather see machine-made fringing on a rug than see damage going further to the pile as a result of no fringe at all.

Attaching machine-made fringing to a rug is one of the simplest tasks to carry out at home, and is a quick and inexpensive repair. Machine-made fringing can only be sewn to a rug when there is kilim work at the damaged end. Under

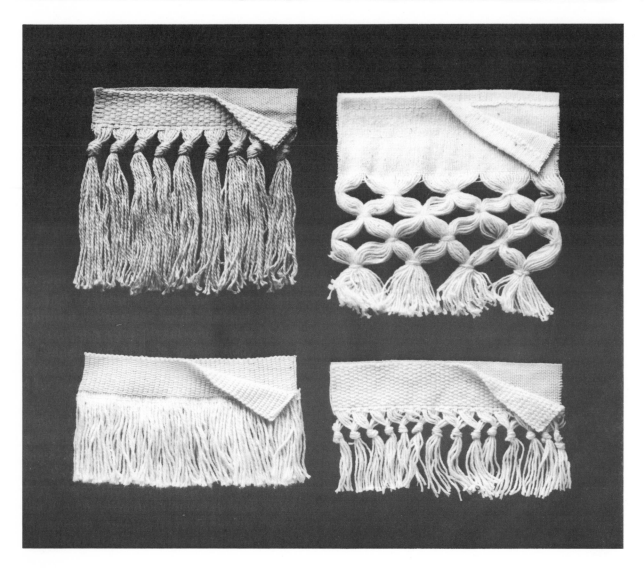

no circumstances should it be attached to the piled part of the rug, nor should the kilim end be trimmed to where the knots begin. Cutting the kilim ends will reduce the value of the rug considerably and will rapidly cause serious damage as gradually the knots unknot. Machine-made fringing is attached as follows:

● Select a machine-made fringe which matches the rug in colour and cut it an inch (2.5 cm) longer than the width of the rug.
● Lay the rug on a flat surface, pile downwards and the back of the rug facing upwards. Insert the kilim end of the rug between the two flaps of the machine-made fringing, leaving ½ inch (1.3 cm) of the fringing protruding at either end, and pin in position. Do not insert the piled part of the rug.
● Neaten the edge of the new fringe by turning back the overlap at one end only and secure by oversewing as shown in the diagram.
● With a threaded needle, sew the rug and fringing together with a firm stabbing stitch, making sure that the sides are well secured. Ensure that the needle passes through both flaps of the fringing and also the rug. Secure the other side edge of the fringing.

The importance of sewing cannot be over-emphasized with regard to such fringing; glue should never be used. If a rug has machine-made fringing glued at the ends, this will reduce its value drastically and the owner will have difficulty if he wishes to resell the rug in the future.

If, for some reason, neither of the two methods of repairing damaged or missing fringes can be carried out, the ends of the rug should be 'stopped' by oversewing, in order to prevent the damage from going further. This is explained in detail in the section of the book dealing with the selvedge or kilim ends on the following pages.

There are many designs of machine-made fringes available for use on oriental rugs. The use of short, strong cotton fringes, made to a simple design, is always preferable, although the wide choice of finish gives plenty of scope for individual taste. These fringes are usually sold by large shops specializing in curtain or soft furnishing supplies.

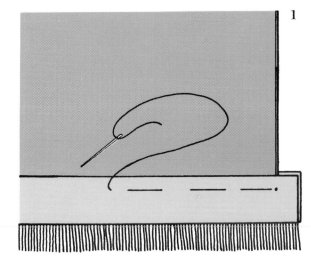

Position the kilim end in the pocket of the machine-made fringe with tacking stitches.

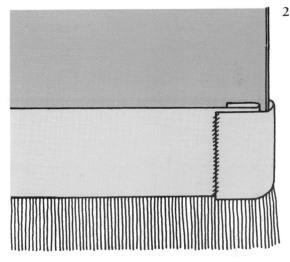

Neaten up the surplus fringe at the sides of the rug by turning it back.

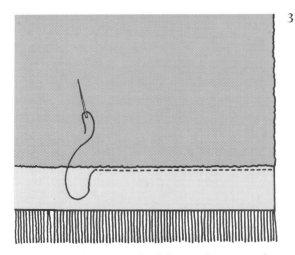

Attach the fringe to the kilim end using a firm, even and closely spaced stabbing stitch.

Selvedge or kilim ends

After the warp threads have been strung on the loom, the first stage in rug making is the weaving of the kilim ends or selvedge. This is achieved by weaving a weft thread in and out of the taut warp threads which, when beaten down with a heavy metal comb, form the kilim ends.

The kilim ends vary in length from rug to rug and weaver to weaver. In some Isfahan and Tabriz rugs there are not more than five beaten rows of weft threads, forming a kilim end of less than $\frac{1}{4}$ inch (0.6 cm). In Kashan rugs, it can be up to $\frac{1}{2}$ inch deep (1.3 cm). With some tribal rugs – such as Baluchi and Kurdish – the kilim ends can become a major part of the rug, stretching for 6 inches (15 cm) or more, and incorporating different coloured weft threads which form a pattern.

Like the fringe, the kilim end acts as a protective barrier. When one of the weft threads in the kilim work begins to work loose, there is cause for alarm. One by one, the weft threads will break away from the rug until the actual knotted pile is reached. This in turn will begin to disappear, knot by knot, row by row, causing serious damage.

Repairing Loose Kilim Ends
If the threads of the kilim ends of a rug are loose and starting to break away, they should

Blanket stitching to secure the kilim end. Contrasting colour is only used here for clarity.

immediately be secured in position by oversewing with a thin, strong, matching coloured thread. Oversewing or blanket stitching, the simple stitches known to all, are perfectly satisfactory.

Should many weft threads already be loose they should be removed carefully, as far as the last line of solid and secure weft threads. Even if there is only one row of weft threads remaining, this should be preserved at all costs. Then, oversew the ends, using a thin, strong thread comparable to that already used in the rug and matching it colourwise to the existing weft threads. Use a diagonal oversewing stitch, sliding the needle along the warp threads.

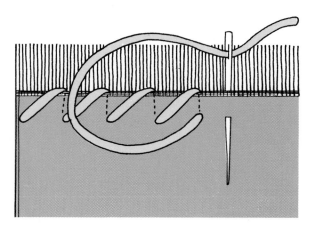

Simple oversewing to secure the last weft thread and prevent the knots disintegrating.

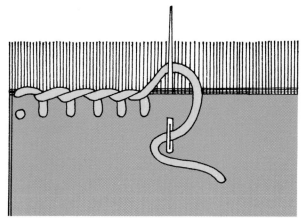

Blanket stitch is a simple variation used to secure the ends of rugs with woollen wefts.

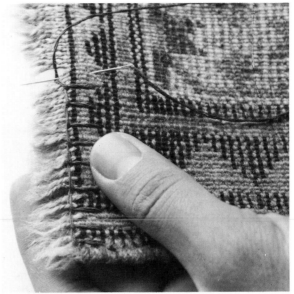

Removing loose or disintegrating knots before securing the last row of weft threads.

Blanket stitch secures the last row of weft threads and is always worked from the back.

Repairing a Rug with No Kilim Ends
When there is no kilim end left at all, the weft threads are loose and the knots are already beginning to disappear, the situation is more serious and needs the following prompt action:

● Carefully remove any knots which are loose, until there is an undamaged and complete weft thread passing on top of a row of knots. Remove only the loose knots, preserving as much of the rug as possible.

● Secure this weft thread in position by sewing over it and also through two or three rows of knots. There are many stitches that can be used for this process, but the easiest and most suitable are blanket stitch or oversewing. The depth of the stitch should be two or three rows of knots and the gap between the stitches should be approximately every two or three knots. In rugs with a woollen weft (like Baluchi, Afghan, Shiraz and some Pakistani), it is preferable to use blanket stitch or loop stitch as this forms an additional guard to the more easily breakable wool fibre. Where a cotton weft is present (like in Hamadan, Isfahan and Heriz rugs) oversewing could be used as cotton is a stronger fibre.

From the aesthetic point of view and also for the protection of the rug, the stitches sewn for this securing process should not be evident on the face of the rug.

Where a rug has no fringe, no kilim end and a considerable amount of pile has started to come away from the rug in an irregular shape, it is advisable to stitch the rug as already mentioned, but following the shape of the damage. There is no need to attempt to even the end of the rug by removing all the rows of knots until straight. If you find this unevenness unattractive, it is advisable to take the rug to a dealer who will advise as to whether it would harm the rug to remove the remaining pile and even up the end of the rug; or whether it would be better to reweave the damaged area; or stop it as it is. The value of the rug will determine the course of action to be taken.

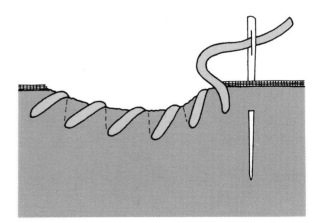

Simple oversewing of any disintegration prevents the damage making further inroads.

89

$\mathcal{S}$*ide cords*

In most oriental rugs, the side cords are formed by two or more warp threads additionally bound and secured by the weft threads. As the rug is knotted row by row, so the weft thread secures the knots and binds the cords. On most rugs, the side cords have an extra woollen binding besides the weft threads. The side cords have no resilient pile and, acting as the exterior guards to the rug, they receive constant wear and tear; therefore, side cords will often be the first areas requiring attention.

Damaged side cords are not a cause for concern provided action is taken immediately. If left unrepaired, the cords may break away completely from the rest of the rug and, with the pile unprotected, the knots will then fall away. Side cord repair is common and does not affect the value of the rug; in fact, almost all rugs at some stage undergo one or several side cord repairs during their lifetime.

The simple process of overbinding the side cords is the first repair most rugs require.

Side cords should be checked regularly and carefully, for they may often be damaged without appearing so. Damage to side cords is usually progressive and can be broken into three stages; the first two can be attended to at home and the third needs professional attention.

Repairing Damaged Binding
This is a minor repair job and one of the easiest for the inexperienced layman to tackle. In this example, the side cord foundation (the warp threads) is perfectly sound and only its binding is loose, unsecured, worn or broken. To repair this binding:

● Select a matching colour wool thread and a strong needle. Secure the thread by running it through the side cord.
● Rebind the side of the rug with circular oversewing stitches.
● In certain rugs, the cords are bound twice. To rebind the cords of such rugs, use a figure-of-eight stitch. It is important that the start and finish of the new binding is properly secured and that the old binding does not unfurl; this should be stabilized by overbinding.

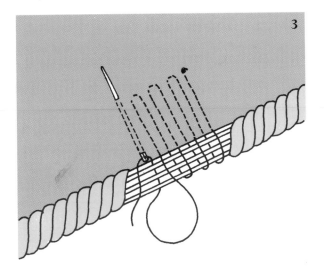

To repair damaged side cords first trim the ends of the broken warp threads.

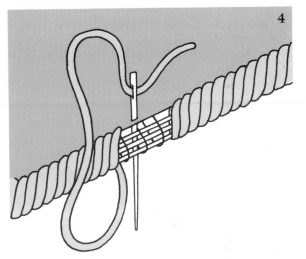

Reinsert the appropriate number of warp threads, making the tension firm but not too tight.

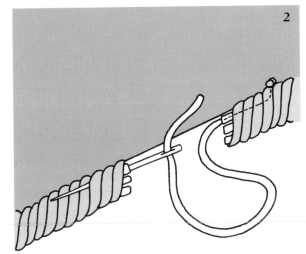

Without disturbing their tension, loop the newly-inserted weft threads into bundles.

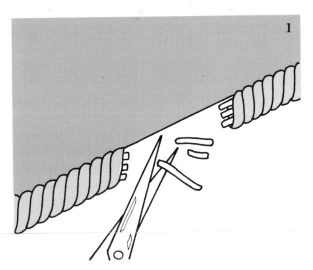

Matching the colour and quality of the original, overbind the new side cord.

Repairing Partly Damaged Side Cords

Here, in addition to damaged binding, the actual cords themselves are broken in one or two places; therefore, the broken original warp threads forming the cord foundation need to be joined by new threads before they can be bound. The repair should be carried out as follows:

● With sharp scissors, trim the ends of the broken cord warp threads to leave a clean cut.
● With a needle threaded with a fibre of comparable thickness, quality, strength and colour to the warp, join the two broken ends of the same cord together. Do not pull the new thread too tightly or leave it too loose – allow it to lie straight. Secure the thread by passing it at least $\frac{1}{2}$ inch (1.3 cm) through the centre of the old thread. Return the needle through the centre of the other warp threads and repeat to form as many warp threads as originally required, before securing. Add the weft threads.
● Rebind the new cord by oversewing.

As the side cords are different on the rugs made in different areas, the method of over-binding should be governed by the way it was originally made. Rugs made in the Isfahan area, such as Najaf-Abad rugs, have a single binding, but in some rugs made in Tabriz and in some Caucasian rugs, there is a double binding in the form of a figure-of-eight. In some

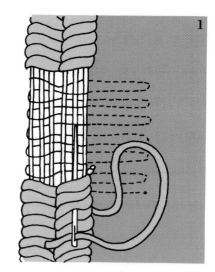

Never neglect early side-cord damage or the deterioration may need professional attention.

Doubly-bound side cords are repaired like singly-bound cords, up to the overbinding stage.

Kurdish or Baluchi rugs there are three or more bindings.

The simplest and easiest overbinding is the single side cord, as seen on page 25. In double side cords, the binding should be done over and under two bunches of warp threads, following the figure-of-eight shown in the diagrams. When restoring the binding on one side of the rug, the colours on the matching unbroken side of the rug should be copied.

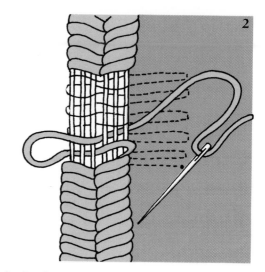

Here the binding goes over and under two bundles of warps, forming a figure-of-eight.

Badly Damaged or Missing Side Cords

When the majority of the side cord is broken or even entirely missing, the damage may already extend to the piled borders of the rug. There are two ways to repair this severe damage. The most complete restoration job would involve the reweaving of the missing portion of the border, reinsertion of the missing cords and then binding; this would probably have to be done by a professional restorer. The second, less time-consuming and considerably cheaper short cut would call for the cutting of part or all of the damaged border and side cords and sewing a ready-made bound side cord to the rug.

As both these methods are lengthy processes and require meticulous precision, it is not advisable for the layman to attempt them himself. The continued protective function in cases of such grave side cord damage can only be assured by a professional repair job. The layman can, however, effectively stop further damage even by the crudest oversewing.

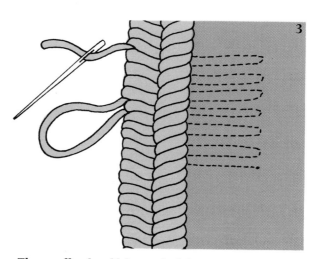

The needle should be pushed horizontally through the overbinding to finish it off.

Curling edges

The term 'curling' means that the sides of the rug do not lie flat on the floor but curl under the rug, thus forming a small ridge. Curling rarely occurs with loosely knotted rugs, but certain types of rugs are particularly susceptible to this problem: some Bidjar, Qum, Kashan, Isfahan, fine modern Tabriz and frequently Sarouk rugs.

The reasons for curling may be either that the weft threads are too tightly inserted and are, therefore, pulling, or that the weft thread is made from an overspun fibre which contracts after a period and pulls.

Curling looks unsightly and if not treated promptly will lead to excessive wear along the ridges. Treatment for most rugs is by one of two methods, both of which can be carried out successfully at home. The first method is the simpler, though less enduring, repair of the two.

This first method involves attaching a strip of thin linoleum or leather underneath each side of the rug as follows:

● Obtain a strip of linoleum or leather approximately 1½ inches (3.8 cm) in width and cut to the exact length of the rug (excluding kilim ends and fringes).
● Lay the rug on a flat surface, pile downwards, with the back of the rug facing upwards.

● Using a very strong needle and a thick, string-like thread, sew the strip to the back of the rug along one side. Sew it with a large, herring-bone stitch. These large stitches will be visible on the back of the leather or linoleum strip but the catch stitches that join the strip to the rug should be very small and should not show through the pile on the front of the rug.

This method should rectify the problem, but the rug will only stay uncurled while the strip is in place; removal of the strip will result in curling once again. This strip sewn to the sides of the back of the rug does not harm the rug and in no way affects its value.

The second solution to the curling problem is more time-consuming and difficult but it does provide a life-long cure. It is the only suitable method where the highest standard of workmanship is desired and, therefore, is in many cases left to professionals. However, it can be undertaken by the keen and patient amateur.

● Lay the rug on a flat surface with the pile downwards and the back of the rug facing upwards. Select a fairly thin but strong thread, matching the colour to that of the selvedge binding.
● Take the curling edge and, with one hand, hold it flat. Starting at one end of the rug and approximately 1 inch (2.5 cm) in from the side of the rug, insert a medium-sized threaded needle through the lines and knots at a diagonal angle until the side cords are

1

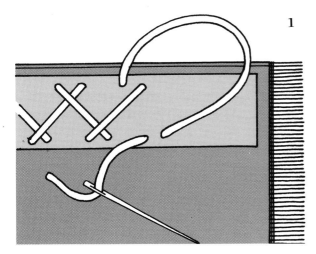

Attaching a thin, supportive strip to the back of a curling edge using herring-bone stitch.

2

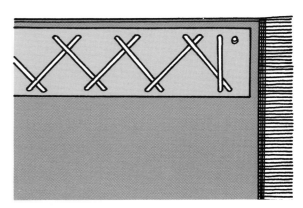

If the strip has been sewn on properly, the rug will lie flat without puckers or ridges.

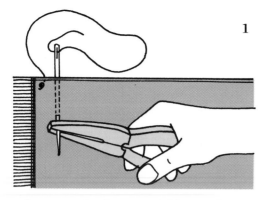

Curling edges can also be corrected by sewing through side cords to a 1-inch depth.

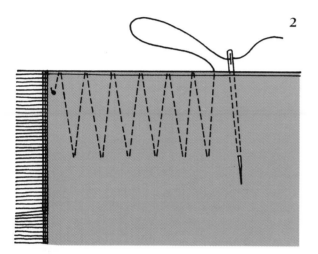

It is essential to keep the tension of the zig-zag stitching even, to prevent puckering.

What Not To Do

Never glue the curled edge of the rug to the floor.

Never glue any material or binding to the curled edge; this will provide a very short-term solution, for after a period the glued material will come apart from both rug and binding and the rug will have suffered permanent damage; and its value will also have decreased.

Never apply hot wax to the curling edge — another short-term solution which, in the long run, will cause dirt and grit to be absorbed, making the rug hard, dry and brittle and damaging the warp and weft.

Never nail the curled edges to the floor or sew them to your machine-made fitted carpeting. This will eventually rip and tear the rug and will not cure the curling problem.

Ironing the curled sides with a hot iron and damp cloth is a solution often suggested. This will solve the problem for a short time, but the heat of the iron will damage the foundation of the rug and this method is therefore **not** recommended.

reached. A small pair of grooved, nose-tip pliers will help to push the needle through. The thread should be pulled tightly enough to keep the working area completely flat, straightening out the curl. Pulling this new thread too tightly will make the rug curl in the opposite direction; too loosely will leave it in its present curled state.

● Continue this process along the entire side of the rug, leaving two rows of knots between each line of thread inserted.

● Complete the other side of the rug in the same way.

If you do not wish to repair the curled edges of a rug by either of the methods described and cannot locate a professional to do the work, the rug should be used in a place where it will not get a lot of wear, like, for example, a bedroom, or a study, so that the raised ridges will not receive excessive wear.

In some rugs, sewing through the side cords may require pliers to draw the needle.

Repiling

When the repiling of a worn area has been completed, the tufts of new pile should be trimmed down to match the original.

The term repiling means the replacement of lost, badly damaged or worn knots and the reinsertion of the pile. With patience this can be done at home; the amount of patience and time required depends on the size of the damaged area and the fineness of the weave in the rug to be repaired.

Damage to the pile can be made by moths, continual traffic on one or two parts of the rug resulting in wear, or by fire.

Moths usually devour the woollen parts of oriental rugs; where the warp, weft and pile are all of wool the moth will eat through them completely, leaving a hole. If the foundation is of cotton, the damage will only extend as far as the pile. With the cotton warp and weft sound and strong, this can be repiled.

Rugs in use on the floor often receive heavy wear in one or two particular areas, due to their continual exposure. These areas will, therefore, show signs of wear earlier than the rest of the rug. A common occurrence is the wearing of a rug around the legs of a dining-room table, yet the centre of the rug remains in good condition.

Rugs can need repairing as a result of burn damage from cigars or cigarettes and burnt cinders from an open wood or coal fire. Rugs with a thick pile obviously receive less damage than those with a short nap. If the burn has only singed the very uppermost ends of the pile and the knot basically remains intact, the burnt tips of the fibres should be trimmed with curved scissors. This will leave the trimmed area with a slightly lower length of pile than the rest of the rug, but this does not matter as it does not normally affect the beauty or stability of the rug. However, if the burn has damaged the actual base of the knots, this area will have to be cleaned of the damaged knots and new ones will have to be reinserted. Where the burn is even more serious and the warp and weft threads have been destroyed by fire, this will require the reinsertion of new warp and weft threads before the repiling process can be executed (see the section dealing with repairing a hole on page 99).

How to Repile

To carry out a lasting repiling job, it is essential that the warp and weft (the foundation) be firm, undamaged and in good condition. Damaged warp or weft threads cannot support the insertion of new knots and must therefore be replaced.

Rugs must first be cleaned before repiling is carried out. If the pile is not cleaned first and then is cleaned after repiling, the yarns, which once matched, will no longer match, for the original likeness in colour was made with a dirtied colour.

Natural fibres, like wool and silk, of comparable colour, quality and age should be selected for the replacement of the pile. Man-made fibres should not be used even if they provide the perfect colour match. Matching the fibres should be done in a natural light as fluorescent light distorts the shading. There are usually good selections of yarns at specialist wool or needlework shops and there are even certain shops that sell vegetable-dyed wools. It is worthwhile taking time over the selection of the matching fibres as a well-matched yarn is one of the secrets of an invisible repiling job. Repiling should be carried out as follows:

● Remove the remains of any knots left within the damaged area. Moths usually digest the wool from the front (but sometimes the back) of the rug, but part of the knot will remain trapped between the warp and weft threads. Particles of damaged knots will also remain in the cases of wear or burns. Remove the damaged or partly damaged knots by inserting a needle from the front of the rug between the warp and weft threads and the remainder of

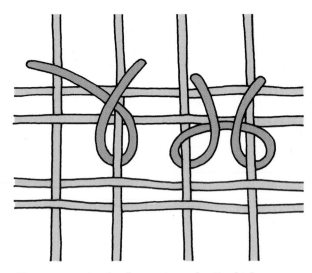

Two stages in the formation of a Turkish or Ghiordes knot, used when repiling with a needle.

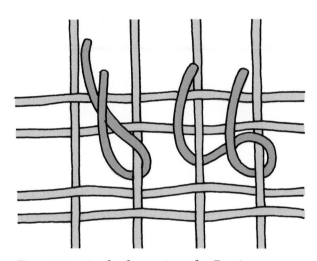

Two stages in the formation of a Persian or Senneh knot used when repiling with a needle.

the knot will then fall away at the back.

● Determine whether the type of knot used on the rug is Persian or Turkish as the new knot should match the original knot.

● With a threaded needle or hook re-knot the pile into the damaged area with the correct knot. Following the colour and design is made easy by following the design of a similarly patterned area elsewhere in the rug (often at the opposite end as many rugs are symmetrical). Examine the similar design from the back and count the number of knots used in each colour per horizontal line, for example, two blue, three red, two blue, four brown and so on. With the correct colour for each stitch, work horizontally in the same manner. As each knot is reinserted, leave the loose threads about

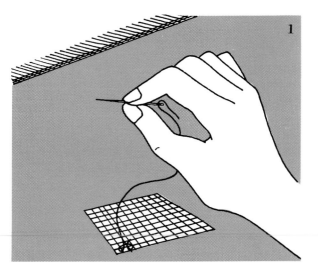

½ inch (1.3 cm) longer than the rest of the pile.
● When the damaged area has been completely repiled, it should be lightly ironed from the back with a warm (not hot) iron in order to settle the newly-knotted pile into position.
● With a pair of curved scissors (nail scissors are ideal) carefully and evenly trim the longer threads to the same height as the rest of the pile of the rug.

Repiling is an easy repair to carry out. Patience and common sense are all that are needed and using the above method the results are most satisfying. Repiling is a true 'life saver', adding years to the life of a rug. The pile covers the bare foundation of the rug and prevents it from disintegrating.

When starting to knot, the direction of new pile should follow that of the old.

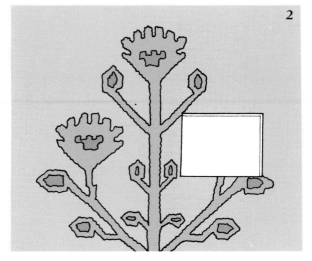

The pattern for a repiling repair should be taken from the opposite side of the rug.

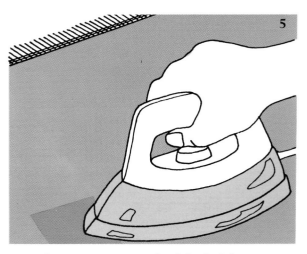

Use a magnifying glass to count the knots on the back of the patterned area to be copied.

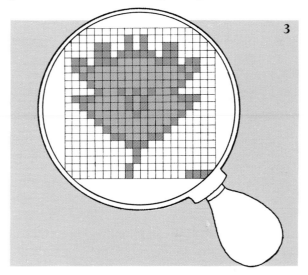

Trimming down a newly knotted area to make the pile the same height as the original.

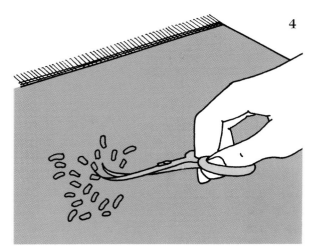

A repiling repair is completed by lightly pressing it from the back to set the knots.

Repairing Designs

The rug restorer's experienced eye alone has developed an instinct for replacing knots with accuracy of colour and design to make the repiling job an undetectable repair. For the layman, a little extra help will be required in order to achieve the same professional result.

As most rugs consist of various similar designs repeated to form one complete work, it is usually possible to locate an identical design to the damaged section elsewhere on the rug. After examining this undamaged design section (of approximately the same size as the area to be repiled) from the back of the rug, take a piece of graph paper and, with each small printed square representing a single knot, mark on the paper with corresponding colours each knot of the design – eg 1 red, 2 blue, 3 white, etc. Transfer the rug design to the paper accurately row by row and this will then visually act as the repiling guide. A colour-charted graph such as this is prepared by an artist at the inception of a new rug and it is to this that the weavers periodically refer when knotting their design. An illustration of an artist preparing a rug design on squared paper may be seen on page 25.

Select an area of the rug in which a similar design can be clearly distinguished from the back. The knots can then be counted, the colour noted and transferred to graph paper.

Cheating by Painting

Although repiling is a comparatively easy job, it is somewhat time-consuming, especially with a finely-knotted rug. Certain dealers in search of a quick sale may avoid a lengthy repiling job by disguising the worn area of a rug by 'painting' it with a felt-tipped pen. This painting process, when the paint is expertly applied, can make the rug look as if it is in excellent condition. Close examination will be required by the untrained eye in order to detect this 'cheating', but a trained eye will immediately locate the painted area in a rug.

Painting does not actually harm a rug if the paint used is colour fast. A non-fast paint would cause colour run when wetted. A painted area in a rug will only look good for a very limited period of time, after which the paint will wear off and the warp and weft threads will be re-exposed as a bare, worn area. Even though painting might not be harmful to a rug, it is not to be recommended.

Repairing holes

Holes occur as the result of a variety of mishaps such as burns, spilt acid and moth attack etc. These holes may have started as small slits and if left unrepaired will have grown. Any hole should be repaired as soon as possible; the sooner the repair is carried out, the easier the job and the more successful the final result.

Most holes can be repaired at home, with the exception of very large ones, for it would be difficult for the layman to match the design of the pile accurately over a large area. Holes in silk and antique rugs should not be tackled by the layman either as these need special handling as the fibres are so delicate.

Different methods are used for repairing holes, depending on the type of rug and the extent of the damage. The easiest and most common way is first to reweave the warp and weft threads; thus replacing the foundation of the rug, and then to reinsert a series of new knots, in other words to repile.

Reweaving the Foundation
Check the damaged area to see what fibre or fibres have been used for the warp and the weft threads. Some rugs such as Shiraz and Afghan use wool for both warp and weft. Other rugs like Hamadan or Nain use cotton for the warp and weft. Certain Isfahans have silk warp threads but cotton weft threads; whereas various Caucasian and Pakistani examples have cotton warp threads and wefts of wool. It is essential that corresponding yarns be selected with which to insert the new foundation. The yarn should be of the same weight as the existing threads. Only pure, natural fibres must be used, not nylon threads or mixtures with nylon.

● Remove the damaged and partly damaged knots from the immediate surrounding area of the hole to be repaired, but take care to remove no more than is absolutely necessary.
● Trim the damaged warp and weft threads, leaving a clean hole on which the work can be carried out. Take care not to tidy the hole into a circle but into a shape with angles.
● Lay the rug on a flat surface, a table or the floor can be used; pile of the rug downwards and the back of the rug facing upwards. The insertion of the foundation is carried out from the back of the rug.
● Match the new thread in thickness and colour to the existing warp thread. Thread a needle and knot the end of the thread. Reweave the warp threads first by starting at one side

When mending a hole, the debris of loose knots should first be cleared away.

The damaged warp and weft threads should be neatly trimmed away leaving an angular hole.

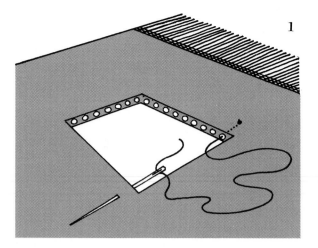

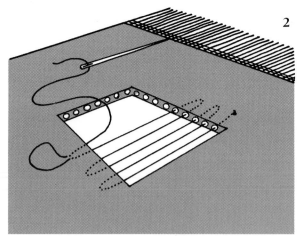

Inserting the first warp thread through the knot from the back of the rug.

Returning the needle through the knots to reinsert all the warp threads.

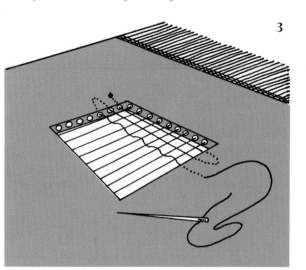

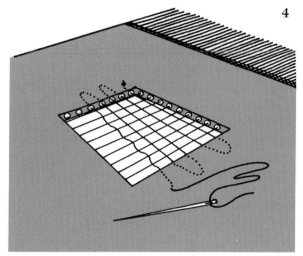

Inserting the new weft threads under and over each warp thread.

Inserting all the correctly tensioned weft threads to make a new foundation for repiling.

of the hole and passing the threaded needle vertically through the back of the firm knots from one side of the hole through to the other side. The needle should be passed through about $\frac{1}{2}$ inch (1.3 cm) of firm undamaged warp thread on either side of the hole to secure it. If it is difficult to pass the needle through the rug then pliers can be used to push and pull the needle through. It is important that the two corresponding broken warp threads be rejoined to one another, making sure that the vertical stitch through the un-damaged area passes through one side of the single knot. Return the needle with a parallel stitch, rejoining the adjacent warp thread, passing the needle through the other side of the knot. Continue until all the new warps are

rewoven. Do not pull the newly inserted threads too tightly or leave them untaut. The tension should be firm but should not create puckers.

● After reinserting all the missing warp threads, insert the weft threads in the same way but with horizontal stitches passing in and out of every warp thread.

● Repile this 'canvas', matching the fibre, design and colours as explained in the repiling section on page 98.

The correct insertion of the new foundation of the rug is vital to the success of repairing a hole correctly. It is this foundation that holds the new knots in place and a solid foundation will make the repiling process even easier.

Patching

Sometimes when a rug has been mistreated badly a hole, which could once have been repaired quite easily, becomes so enlarged and the rug so damaged that the cost of reweaving the foundation and re-knotting the pile would be too great in relation to the value of the rug. In such cases the only solution is the repair known as 'patching up' — the sewing of another piece of handmade rug (the patch) into the hole.

Patching serves to strengthen and protect the badly damaged rug. It will stop the damage going further and will enable the rug to be used again, rather than being discarded. Deciding whether a rug needs reweaving or patching requires common sense. If in doubt as to which method to use, consult a rug specialist.

Compared with reweaving and repiling, patching is a relatively simple job and can easily be done at home — once a matching handmade patch has been found. The patch should come from a rug of the same region and should be of a comparable colour, pattern, quality and age. Of course, it is impossible to find the exact match, but try and find as near a match as possible. A selection of rug pieces is needed in order to find a suitable patch, and your local rug repairer or dealer will probably be able to help.

Having chosen the patch, this now has to be inserted as follows:

● Tidy the damaged area by removing the loose and damaged knots from around the hole; only remove what is absolutely necessary and preserve as much as is possible. Follow the shape of the damaged area and leave the hole with angled corners. Rounded edges are not desirable as the patch cannot be properly secured.

● Cut the patch to the exact size of the tidied hole, by placing the patch under the hole and drawing around the hole, making sure that the warp and weft of both the rug and the patch are well aligned. The nap of the pile of both pieces must run in the same direction.

● Place the rug on a flat surface, pile facing downwards. Place the patch in position in the hole and place a small empty bottle under the patch to raise it and the rug, making joining easier.

● Sew the patch in place from the back of the rug, sewing the warp threads first and then the weft threads.

● Lightly iron the sewn area of the patch on the back of the rug over a damp cloth with a warm iron to eliminate any puckers.

Patching is a very uncommon method of repair and it is usually inadvisable except in the most desperate circumstances where no other method of restoration is feasible. This repair can be seen in some sixteenth and seventeenth-century museum pieces such as the Ardebil.

Remove loose knots and trim stray warp and weft threads to leave a tidy angular hole.

Place the piece of matching rug under the hole and mark round it with tailor's chalk.

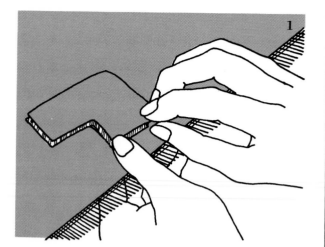

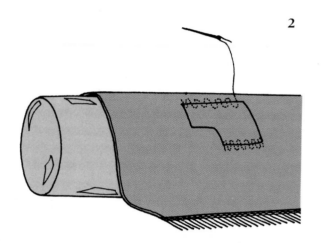

Place the prepared patch in position in the hole, making sure that its pile runs in the same direction as that of the rug.

Place an empty bottle or round hard object under the patch as a support and then sew the warp threads of the patch and rug together.

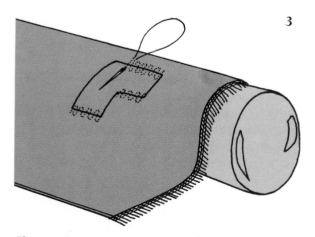

Change the direction of the bottle and sew through the weft threads of patch and rug. Ensure the corners of the patch are secure.

What Not To Do

The worst thing that can be done with a patch is to glue or tape it to the rug. A glued rug is the restorer's nightmare for when the glue or glue-backed tape dries it makes the foundation of the rug hard and brittle and, over a period of time, will form splinters which will cut into the foundation of the rug. Dried glue on a rug makes a sewing repair impossible, as a needle cannot be inserted through the knots and foundation which are hard and inflexible.

Cutting and Joining

In the past, when a runner was too long for a hall or a rug too large for a room, it was acceptable that the rug be reduced in size by cutting it in order to make it fit within the limitations of the room. Such action was carried out on the recommendation of people who knew and cared little about the preservation of oriental rugs. Even today this process is still in use.

Sadly, many fine and antique handmade rugs have been cut and joined in order to accommodate furniture, fireplaces and in order to fit into small rooms. Such ill-fated rugs have been regarded as no more than a cheap piece of carpeting, altered to suit a man-made need. Cutting and joining an oriental rug should **never** be done. Not only is the life span of the rug reduced, but it also slashes its value.

Reducing the size of a rug is only advised in extenuating circumstances, such as when the rug has a very large hole, has disintegrated partly and is so badly damaged that reweaving, repiling, and even patching are out of the question. It should be stressed that this situation — and only this — is the sole occasion to cut and join a rug, thus enabling the rug to survive at all. Having established that cutting and joining is the only solution to save a rug, then the work should be carried out only by an expert rug restorer.

$\mathcal{S}$plits and tears

The splitting or tearing of a rug is usually the result of general carelessness or mishandling — perhaps the rug is finely knotted with a brittle warp and weft and it has been folded (instead of rolled); or possibly the rug was pulled over a sharp, metal stair edge; maybe the jagged lifting device of a fork-lift truck split the packaging in which the rug was enclosed and damaged the rug; or even a hook could have penetrated the rug during shipment. Splits and tears need not cause irreparable damage if attended to immediately.

Splits are of three types: the vertical split in which only the weft is damaged; the horizontal split in which only the warp is damaged; and the diagonal split in which both the warp and weft are damaged.

When the split is fresh, the majority of knots usually remain in position and the repair is relatively simple to carry out at home. When the split is old and has been left unrepaired, there are often numerous knots missing and then the split has to be repaired in the same way as a hole would be repaired (see page 99).

Vertical Tears
This is the easiest of the three splits to repair as only the weft threads are broken while the warp threads and pile are normally still sound and intact.

● Place the rug on a flat surface, pile downwards. Place a reasonably strong, small cylinder horizontally (an empty bottle is ideal), under the torn area. This forms a small ridge on which to work.
● Select a strong thread of the same colour and thickness as the weft. The size of the needle and strength of the thread is determined by the fineness of the rug. Wax the thread.
● Starting two or three rows below the tear, begin to join the broken weft threads together by sewing a new thread through each line. Pull it taut. The width of the stitches either side of the damaged area varies from rug to rug, but should not be less than three lines of knots; only sew as far as is needed in excess of three lines in order to leave the rug secure.

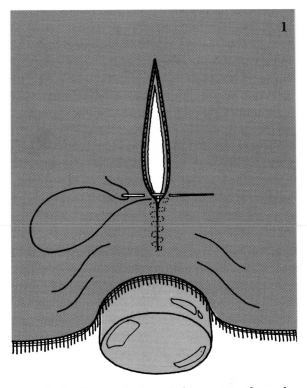

Join the broken weft threads by sewing through each line of them. Ensure each row of knots stays in its original alignment.

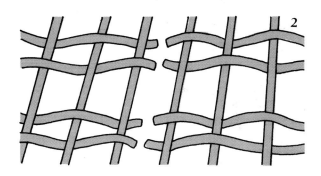

As a guideline, the finer the rug, the shorter the stitch: the coarser the rug, the longer the stitch. As the new weft thread is sewn, it should pass in and out of the firm warp threads.
● Remove the bottle and with the rug flat and in the same position, iron the repaired area with a warm (not hot) iron on the back of the rug only. This will eliminate any puckers.

Horizontal Tears
With the horizontal tear, it is the warp threads that are damaged and broken, and the weft threads normally remain unaffected. This repair is slightly more difficult than a vertical repair as the new warp thread to be inserted has to pass twice through each individual knot

103

A horizontal tear with broken warp threads.

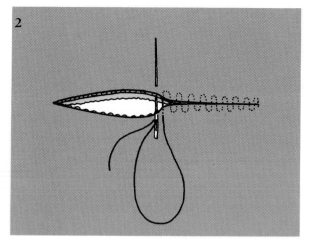

Sewing through the eyes of each knot.

(as the original warp threads did). The repair should be carried out as follows:

● Lay the rug flat on a table, pile downwards. Lay an empty bottle or round cylinder horizontally under the split as a support. Join the two broken ends of the warp threads by sewing with a matching thread.
● The threaded needle is inserted from a minimum of three rows of knots below the tear and is passed through one side (or eye) of the knot and through a further minimum three rows of knots on the other side of the tear. Pull the thread tight enough to close the slit, but not to cause puckers. Return the needle parallel to the first stitch, passing it through the other side of the same knot. It is important that the warps be carefully matched and that the new thread passes through the

knots in the same way as the rug was originally made.
● Continue sewing the new warp threads in this manner along the entire length of the split, carefully securing each knot with two warp threads.
● On completion, lightly press with a warm (not hot) iron to eliminate any puckers.

Diagonal Tear
When a diagonal tear occurs, the warp threads and weft threads are both damaged. Provided no knots are missing, this can be repaired by reinserting new warp threads and joining the broken ones and then reweaving the weft threads. Repairing a diagonal tear requires much patience and delicacy of touch and those with clumsy fingers should not be tempted to test their skills with this repair.

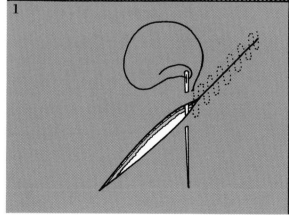

When mending a diagonal tear, sew through the warp threads first.

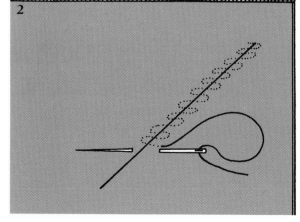

The weft threads are then sewn through to complete the repair.

Repairing flat-woven rugs

Kilims, by virtue of their light-weight make-up and lack of pile, are more delicate than pile rugs. For this reason, it is recommended that kilims are not subjected to heavy traffic and are best suited as wall hangings or table coverings where their long-term survival will be assured.

As with pile rugs, the most common areas in need of attention in kilims are sides, ends and corners. As always, but possibly more importantly with kilims as there are but warp and weft threads forming the entire rug, a quick response to any detected damage is essential.

Kilims have different types of finishes at their ends – some have no fringes at all, some a knotted fringe, and some a long straight fringe. If the fringes get damaged, it is best simply to secure the damaged section by firmly oversewing (as explained on page 88, Repairing Loose Kilim Ends) to prevent further fraying. Where there is no fringe at all (and there is often solely a woven surface, sometimes doubled and sewn at the back of the rug), this should be left well alone – no attempt should be made to make a fringe as this will only weaken the warps unnecessarily.

Wear often shows on the protective weaving at the ends and corners and it is vital that this be quickly repaired or it will unravel itself with great rapidity. Oversewing this damaged area neatly and firmly will prevent this.

Repairing Sides of Kilims

As with pile rugs, the sides of kilims are often the first areas to sustain damage. This is because the warp threads forming the sides are often thicker (for the purposes of sturdiness) than the central warps. As they are therefore raised higher than the rest of the rug, the side cords, binding or weft threads receive more wear.

Repairing the sides or selvedges of kilims is simply a matter of returning the weft threads around the warp threads forming the selvedge. The number of selvedge weft threads used varies from kilim to kilim, depending on its

A late nineteenth-century flat-weave saddle bag (4 ft 1 in×2 ft 3 in/127.6 cm×68.6 cm) made by Qashqā'i of the Shiraz region. Bags and animal covers are still produced in considerable quantity by nomadic and village weavers and serve a dual function for storage and tent furnishing.

105

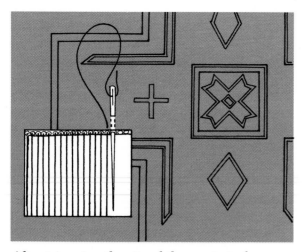

After trimming the site of the repair to form an angular hole, insert the warp threads.

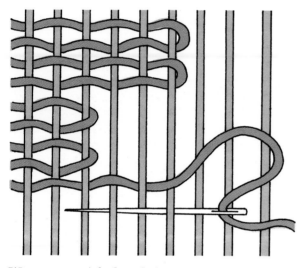

Weave new weft threads by sewing under and over the warp threads.

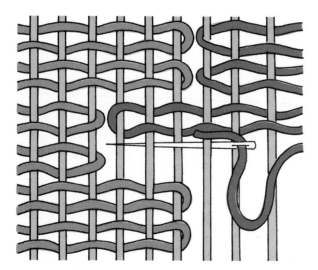

Weaving different coloured weft threads in a kilim to restore the pattern.

origins. Most Caucasian and Anatolian kilims utilize two or three very thick wefts, wrapped around two or three warp threads. In Persian kilims, one, two or three thick warps are used.

This early repair is carried out to the sides of a kilim in the same way as to the sides of a pile rug, as explained on page 91.

Repairing a Hole in a Kilim

A hole in a kilim is possibly more critical than that in a pile rug as there are no knots to protect the foundation — a decorated version of which a kilim in fact is. Obviously, at the first sign of damage, attention should be given to prevent the expansion of the hole.

A hole is repaired in a kilim as follows:

● First the damaged area needs to be tidied by trimming the loose threads to give a clean surface on which to work.
● New warp threads are then reinserted in place of those destroyed as explained on page 100. This is much facilitated with the help of an embroidery frame. By securing the frame around the hole, the correct tension for the new threads will be assured, a very important factor in the successful repair of a kilim hole.
● Keeping the frame in position, the new weft threads should be passed under and over the warps, covering these entirely, in the corresponding coloured threads. It is absolutely necessary to overweave an additional four or five weft threads of the undamaged area in order to properly secure the work.

Typical star motif from a flat-weave textile, drawn on squared paper for reference.

106

Repairing a Sumak (Brocading or Weft Wrapping)

As a sumak is basically a kilim with additional brocading or weft wrapping superimposed upon it, repairs to sumaks are in the first instance the same as those to kilims. The sides and cords may be repaired in an identical way.

Repairing a sumak hole is slightly more difficult as it involves the additional weft wrapping after the foundation has been rewoven as per the previous instructions for a kilim. It is this reweaving of the foundation that forms the canvas on which the brocading can be done:

● First, the brocade threads should be chosen of corresponding colour, quality and fibre as those which are undamaged.

● This thread is then wrapped around three warp threads (2 or 4) and back over two (1 or 3) warp threads, depending on the original manner of weaving (see diagram).

● Following the pattern with colour changes, the stitches should form a continuous chain structure.

When used in the correct interior design setting governed by their delicacy, kilims and sumaks should not incur substantial damage and, therefore, slight repairs can be easily and satisfactorily carried out.

In some kilims and sumaks small areas of damage are not immediately obvious and one should often examine them for signs of wear.

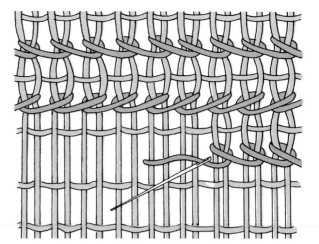

In these diagrams the weft thread goes over four warp threads and back under two.

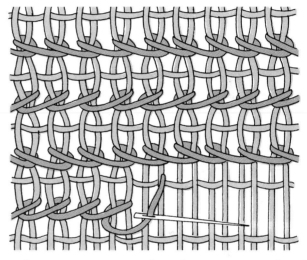

When repairing a sumak, weft wrapping can be done with a needle instead of a weaver's hook.

The first step in repairing a sumak is to prepare a sound foundation.

Overbinding into the foundation, following the colours and method used originally.

Transporting and storing rugs

Storage and transportation are mundane but important facets of the overall care and maintenance of oriental rugs. The disasters that occur due to improper packing, poor shipping, extremes of temperature, dampness and even incorrect folding can all be avoided.

Great care should always be taken in moving a rug from place to place, even when short journeys are involved. Many rugs will split or crack if folded and it is important to adopt the correct method of storage. Rugs can either be folded or rolled and size is often a determining factor as to which process is used and sometimes a combination of the two is best.

Rolling Rugs
Rugs in the following categories should be rolled, never folded:

Finely knotted rugs When a rug feels hard and leathery due to the tightness of knotting, as is the case with Sarouks, Bidjar, Isfahan and Arak rugs, then there is no room for the warp threads to bend between the rows of knots. Folding of such rugs is likely to cause the warp threads to break.

Rugs with warp and/or weft of goat-hair or wool Goat-hair and wool (unlike cotton) do not contract after expansion. By folding certain rugs in this category (Afghan, Shiraz or Baluchi) the warp and/or weft will stretch and if kept folded for any length of time will become misshapen and warped.

Silk rugs Rugs with a silk warp, weft or pile, like Hereke, Tabriz or Qum rugs, are very delicate and the folding of such rugs may break the warp and weft and damage the pile.

Antique rugs Like silk rugs, antique rugs are delicate. Over the years, the warp, weft and knots become rigidly 'set' and folding such rugs may move these out of position. Unlike newer rugs, the foundation and knots of antique rugs do not spring back into shape.

Runners (long, narrow rugs) are normally rolled since their shape lends itself to such treatment.

To roll a rug evenly it is best to use a round, wooden rod or cardboard cylinder (whether it is hollow or not is immaterial as long as it will not break or bend under the weight of the rug to be rolled around it). It should be at least 2 inches (5 cm) longer than the width of the rug. Rugs should be rolled as follows:

● Lay the rug on a clean, flat surface (a table or the floor is ideal depending on the size of the rug), with the pile of the rug facing upwards. It is important that the rug is completely flat as any creases or folds will get 'ironed in' and the rug will be difficult to handle.
● Lay the cylinder or rod on top of the pile at the end at which the weaving of the rug was originally started. This can be ascertained by the direction of the pile or nap; run your hand towards the cylinder and the pile should feel soft and velvety; when you move your hand away from the cylinder, it should feel tougher.
● Roll the rug tightly and evenly around the cylinder. If the rug is over 3 feet (91 cm) wide, it is advisable to have some assistance to assure evenness.
● Tie the rug with string at approximately 12-inch (30-cm) intervals. Tie the string tightly enough to hold the rug in place, but not so tightly that it cuts into the back.

To avoid crushing the pile, very thick piled rugs like Tabriz and Bidjar should be rolled with the pile outwards by laying the rug pile downwards and then rolling as described.

The following rugs may be folded: rugs which are small, pliable and coarsely woven and large rugs where a full width roll is impractical and the rug is not unduly stiff. Rugs should be folded as follows.

How to Fold a Rug
● Lay the rug flat on a clean surface, pile upwards.
● Fold the rug in half lengthwise, pile inwards. If the rug is large fold it again in half the same way. Then fold in half along the other axis (end to end), and again until it is of an easily movable size.

● Alternatively, a rug folded in half or in quarters lengthwise may then be rolled into a short roll. Protect the fringes by folding the rug inwards the first 3 feet (91 cm) at each end, and then roll.

● Thick pile rugs, Kirman, Heriz and Chinese, should be folded with the pile facing outwards to avoid crush marks and lines remaining on the pile, and to prevent excessive strain on the foundation.

Storage

Before a rug is stored, it is essential that it should be absolutely clean, free of dirt and grit and completely dry. To prevent possible moth damage, spray the rug completely both back and front with a proprietary moth spray.

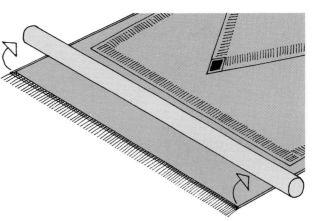

Rolling a rug round a tube, pile inwards.

Carefully fold or roll the rug as recommended and then wrap it in hessian or burlap (or any other strong, natural fibred fabric which will afford a little protection to the rug). Tie with string. *On no account use plastic sheeting if long-term storage is planned.* If a rug is stored in plastic, the live fibres cannot breathe and the resulting rot or moth damage can be disastrous. The only circumstances permitting use of plastic wrapping is where a rug is being transported for a short period of time only.

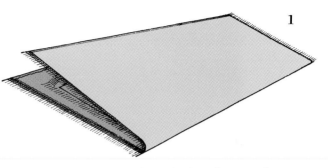

Folding a rug inwards with the pile turned inwards for protection.

It is advisable to store a rug in an area which has some light (in order to discourage moths) and which is completely dry, with no extremes of heat or cold. Normal living conditions are ideal; garages and lofts or attics are unsuitable.

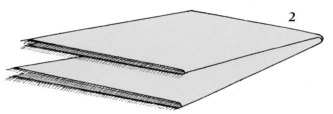

After folding a large rug into quarters, it can then be rolled again.

The rolled or folded packages containing the rugs should be laid flat on the floor, a shelf or on a table, and not stood or leant against an upright object. If possible, they should not be placed one on top of the other, but laid side by side with no other heavy articles on top. If a rug is to be given to a warehouse or storage company for long-term storage, it is important that the above points are explained. Such organizations handle every conceivable object and are not specialists in the field of oriental rugs – if you give no special instructions, your rug will probably be treated in the same way as kitchen equipment or lawnmowers.

Despite all the care taken prior to storage, it is still highly desirable to inspect any stored rug periodically. It is advisable to take the rug out of storage annually and open it out flat in natural light for a day or two. If the weather is fine, outside is best; if not, inside is acceptable. Either hang the rug on a clothes line or fence or better still lay it on a non-porous surface, like a patio. Even if the lawn seems dry, it is not the best place for this airing as there will usually be unseen moisture which the rug will absorb. After a good general inspection and airing, the rug should be resprayed with moth spray and re-rolled or re-folded as before and replaced in the storage area.

If you are fortunate enough to own more rugs than can be used at any one time, use the rugs in rotation. For example, you could use one for six months and then replace it with one that has been in storage.

Part III
The Oriental Rug Market

Whether the intention is to buy or sell, the diversity and exoticism of the oriental rug market can create many pitfalls for the unwary. Dealing with questions of rug purchase, valuation, insurance and re-sale, this section sets down some basic guide-lines for those embarking on this increasingly popular form of domestic investment.

The oriental rug department of a first-rank department store can often provide a selection of fine antique or silk oriental rugs, as well as an abundance of modern handmade pieces.

Buying and Selling Oriental Rugs

*W*hen thinking of buying your first rug, you need to establish your principal purpose, that is, whether you are buying for an investment, collecting, or because you are furnishing your home. If you are an investor you will be concerned most with value and re-sale potential. If you are a collector, intrinsic beauty and rarity would be uppermost in your mind. If, however, you are buying oriental rugs for the purpose of furnishing, then colour, design and the appearance of the rug in the setting of your home are the most important considerations. Whichever category your buying falls into, ultimately it will be affected by your financial means. You must also bear in mind the purpose for which the rug will be used after it has been acquired. Is it to go on the floor, and if so, will it have a lot of wear in an entrance hall, or light wear, as in a bedroom? Or is it to be hung on the wall to be admired but not walked on, or kept in a rug chest to be brought out on special occasions?

Buying for Investment
Runaway inflation has made all fine art objects valuable investments to be considered in much the same way as stocks and shares and real estate. Unlike stocks and shares, they give tangible pleasure and unlike real estate, they are portable. Oriental rugs are one of the few categories of art objects which are truly international and for which a ready demand exists in all developed societies throughout the world. This characteristic means that they are a currency in their own right, and are insulated from the ups and downs attendant upon less specialized art forms. In the East, handmade rugs have traditionally served both as articles of furniture or decoration and as a store of personal wealth. In countries where governments and currencies are often unstable, rugs stand alongside gold as a means by which prosperous citizens provide themselves with a pension in old age.

Old handmade rugs have proved to be an outstanding investment since World War II, and have more than kept up with the rate of inflation. As with all other forms of investment, there can be no certainty that what has increased in value in the past will continue to increase in the future. But handmade rugs are becoming scarce and ever more costly to produce; they have a universal appeal and thus the ingredients of a successful investment remain.

The old adage, that it pays to buy the best you can afford, applies as much to rugs as it does to other commodities; it is doubly important where investment is the prime objective. While any good handmade rug is likely to appreciate in value, some will appreciate faster than others. These are the rugs that are outstanding specimens of their type, costing perhaps twice as much as the average good example. On the whole, antique rugs in good condition are usually a better investment than newly made rugs because of their rarity.

Investment buyers must consider marketability, and they should try to reduce, as far as possible, the margin between buying and selling. The margin is important since the bigger it is the more difficult it is for the investor to recoup his original cost and start again. Specific advice on what to buy is not easy to give, partly because the answer depends largely on personal taste and partly because markets, fashions and relative values change slightly from year to year. Nevertheless, it is advisable to concentrate on buying pieces that are genuinely fine, old and rare. Outstanding rugs for investment are nomadic and village rugs woven in the nineteenth century, especially Caucasian and Turkoman pieces of such origins as Kazak, Kuba, Shirvan and Bokhara. Also worth considering are Persian city rugs of the period 1880–1910, when particularly good rugs were produced in the Kashan, Tabriz, Sarouk and Kirman regions. Apart from these examples, the choice is enormous, and still includes, for those who can afford it, the occasional opportunity of buying a sixteenth- or seventeenth-century 'museum piece'.

As far as modern rugs are concerned, it is a curiosity of the market that even fine examples are often poorly regarded by the trade and by discriminating private buyers until they have acquired the patina of age. When a modern Nain or silk Qum rug comes to be sold by its first owner within the year of purchase, it will normally fetch less than the current wholesale price for an equivalent new piece. It is reasonable to assume that eventually such rugs will gain in value, and to that extent they present an interesting investment opportunity for the buyer who wants something that can be used in the home as well.

An investment buyer who is not himself an expert should always seek expert advice. Most reputable rug dealers will be willing to give free advice, or to buy to order good antique rugs for a modest commission. The international auction houses, as well as some distinguished department stores, employ experts who will give advice normally free of charge to potential purchasers.

The shop of an up-market town dealer, such as this example in London, provides a large, high-quality stock to choose from.

Buying as a Collector

A collector may also be an investor, but his first interest lies in the rugs themselves. The collector will frequently concentrate on a particular type of rug — for example, small Turkoman pieces produced by a particular tribe. A collector will study the subject in depth and will buy and read all available literature on the subject. His aim is to build up a collection which will provide him with at least one example of each subdivision of his subject, and when this is achieved, to increase the quality of his collection by weeding out the poorer specimens and buying nothing but the best.

The established collector is not likely to be in need of advice either on what to buy or how to go about it. In this field personal choice and whim rule the day. As to the novice collector, he may consider some of the following choices: nineteenth-century kilims from Turkey, the Caucasus and Persia; Turkoman storage bag *faces* (known according to size and purpose as *chuvals*, *torbas* and *mafrash*); small Baluchi and Qashqā'i bags and rugs. If the collector is affluent he could set his sights on sixteenth-century Persian and Turkish carpet fragments or early to mid-nineteenth-century Caucasian village rugs of the finest quality. The new collector should always befriend a rug dealer and ask him to look out for examples of what he is seeking.

Furnishing Your Home with Oriental Rugs

Many people do not have the time or the inclination to become 'involved' with rugs, but like to have them about the home to give warmth and create an air of opulence. Rugs in the home are either used for covering the floor or for hanging as a decoration; each purpose requires a different kind of rug: strong and heavy to walk on or light to hang. For hanging, use either your most valuable pieces (provided they are reasonably light in weight and have strong warps) or your old but worn pieces with high-quality designs and colours. Many an antique rug can be rescued from the floor and, when cleaned up, can be given a new lease of life as a wall hanging. When buying, if you cannot afford expensive rugs you should not hesitate to buy cheaper examples from your local rug dealer. For some purposes even a worn 'old wreck' of a carpet will look 'right' and give a few years of service for only a small outlay. Whatever your budget, there will be delightful rugs of some age and quality that you can afford.

Where to Buy

There are several sources available to the private buyer for buying rugs: the local rug dealer, the up-market city dealer, the department store, rug warehouses, the international saleroom, the local saleroom, the one-off auction sale and a private purchase.

The local rug dealer An oriental rug shop will be found in the prosperous areas of most large towns. These shops can be located through telephone directories or the local weekly newspaper. What the local dealer has to offer is a small, but constantly changing stock, and the time and inclination to give personal attention to your requirements, however modest. His prices and profit margins are low because he does not carry a large and expensive stock needing financing on an overdraft, and because he is able to buy a large proportion of his goods from private sources at prices that avoid the middleman's mark-up. If he has bought cheaply he will pass on a share of that benefit to his customer. Again, he is more likely to prefer a quick sale at a low margin than to have to hold stock to gain higher margins.

Cultivate your local dealer, browse in his shop and view his stock. If you have a purchase in mind enlist his help and advice. Tell him what you intend buying and roughly how much you wish to spend. Take him your own rugs for identification and valuation and if they need cleaning or repairing seek his advice — he will either do the work for you or put you in touch with someone who will. If you are hoping to buy something scarce and specialized, he will act as a scout for you.

When buying a rug from a dealer ask him whether he will be prepared to change the rug if you are not satisfied, and ask also whether

Antique Qashqā'i rug (7 ft x 4 ft 5 in/ 184.5 cm x 132.7 cm) showing the distinct rows of small, overlapping botehs, or leaf-like motifs, from which the Paisley design was derived.

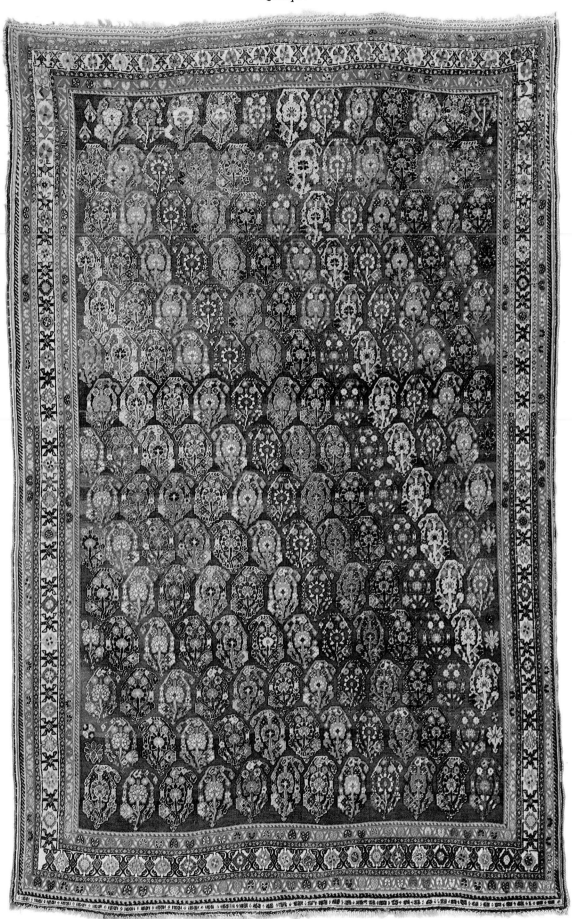

he will be prepared to exchange it in the future. If you are uncertain whether the rug will suit the décor in your home, ask the dealer to bring some pieces to your house or alternatively ask to take the rug home on a few days' approval.

Buying from an established dealer provides one unique advantage over other sources: the right to return pieces that are found to be faulty or damaged. Trust your dealer — it is in his interests that you should be a satisfied customer, and should return to his shop to buy other rugs. It is also in his interest that you should recommend him.

The up-market town dealer Buy from a town dealer if you want the best and the opportunity to choose from a large stock. His goods will be of a superior quality and will be backed by his name and international reputation. Most town dealers are specialists in some type or aspect of oriental rugs and these shops or galleries should be distinguished from those selling nothing but modern pieces, mainly to the tourist trade.

The department store Many of the world's great department stores have an oriental rug department but some have only an oriental rug section within their floor-coverings department. Here it is usual to find a good selection of modern handmade rugs from such origins as China, the Indian sub-continent, Afghanistan and Eastern Europe, with some better quality pieces from Persia. In some rare stores you can find a good selection of fine antique and silk oriental rugs as well. When buying rugs from a department store you will normally get a good rug, pleasant surroundings and excellent service from an attentive staff.

The rug warehouses In London and certain other major capitals of the world, there are specialist warehouses dealing mainly in new oriental rugs. Some are exclusively 'trade', where purchases must be made through a trade agent or intermediary; others, although partly wholesale, also sell direct to the public through advertising. These warehouses are usually situated in the commercial or dockland areas of the city and their overheads are correspondingly reduced. However, because advertising costs are high, their retail prices will not be much lower than their up-market competitors. The private lay buyer may secure a good deal at a warehouse; but he is well advised to patronize only reputable, long-established businesses which provide some kind of a buy-back guarantee.

The auction room If you intend to buy in a saleroom, you must get a copy of the catalogue and visit the saleroom on the day sale goods can be viewed. Always inspect the pieces before the sale. Examine the rug which interests you carefully, looking particularly for signs of the piece having been reduced in size (cut and rejoined); moth damage (especially on the reverse of the rug where in some areas the backs of the knots may have been eaten away); worn areas (sometimes concealed under furniture in the saleroom) and any more extensive damage. Test the rug for rot and brittleness by making a fold of the back of the carpet and bending it. If it makes a cracking noise then it is *churuk* or rotted; also check for splits in the foundation, especially at the centre of the piece. Beware of wrong descriptions in the catalogue: many rugs are described as 'Persian' when they are anything but, and even the greatest salerooms sometimes make mistakes in identification. Beware also of fakes and imitations: sixteenth- and seventeenth-century rugs of great rarity have sometimes been faked in the nineteenth century, and machine-made or Eastern European copies of Persian carpets are frequently found.

Get to the saleroom well before the lot in which you are interested is put up, and take in the atmosphere. Make up your mind beforehand on the price you want to pay and *stick to it*. Do not forget that in most salerooms a buyer's premium of about ten per cent is payable in addition to the hammer price and that value-added tax is payable in some countries on certain goods from trade sources, but this will be indicated in the catalogue. Make clear signals of your bid by flicking your catalogue and nodding your head to the auctioneer. *Stop bidding* when you have reached the maximum price which you would be prepared to pay; if you go on, you may be bidding against another private buyer who has no idea of the true value of the piece, or you may be bidding against a dealer's ring, present in most out-of-town salerooms.

It should be explained that a 'ring' is an illegal though customary practice by which some groups of dealers combine their efforts in the saleroom to buy jointly a rug under price, which is then privately auctioned amongst themselves. Each dealer will only bid against private buyers but not against a member of the ring. The success or failure of such rings depends on the knowledge and expertise of the auctioneer who may advise a reserve price on the article sufficient to prevent it being sold cheaply.

A significant proportion of rugs offered in the salerooms have been entered by dealers, who have varying motives for wishing to dispose of stock in this way. A dealer will often consign a piece to the saleroom if it is unattractive and slow to sell or if there are serious doubts about its condition. If he sells a defective rug to his own customer he will have it returned with attendant damage to his reputation, but if he sells the same piece through the saleroom, there is no recourse on the part of the buyer, who will be deemed to have bought with knowledge of all faults.

Apart from damaged pieces, trade goods are frequently offered at some auctions at high reserve prices in the hope of catching the unwary public.

If you have survived these hazards and have made a successful bid, the auctioneer will take your name and address and you will be required to pay for and remove the rug within a day or two of the end of the sale.

The international salerooms The great international auction houses stage regular, specialist rug sales in London, New York, Zurich and other major centres. The quality of the goods offered and the standard of cataloguing, is normally very high. Here the wealthy private buyer can obtain value for money at the top end of the market, but once again he needs to be an expert or to obtain expert advice beforehand. Even at this level, fakes and imitations slip through the net and vendors can specify reserve prices that are highly speculative. Perhaps the safest approach in these salerooms is to employ the services of an honest expert dealer to advise you or to buy on commission for you.

Provincial salerooms and house contents sales Some provincial auction houses hold occasional specialist rug sales, and some others include rugs with their household goods and antique furniture. Cataloguing is of a variable standard because outside London, New York or other great cities, expertise is comparatively scarce. In all of these salerooms the adage *caveat emptor* — let the buyer beware — applies and the strictures made above apply in full measure.

It is a mistake to expect automatic bargains in local sales — the dealer network is very efficient in sniffing out good rugs in even the remotest and most obscure auction rooms and it is rare indeed for a fine piece to fall into the hands of a private buyer at less than the true value. Beware especially of country house sales and other sales held 'on the premises' in private houses. Because trade and private buyers alike think they are bidding for private goods fresh on the market, competition is keen and prices often show a significant premium over what the same goods would fetch in the permanent saleroom. Occasionally at such sales two determined buyers can engage in a fight to the death that produces a hammer price way above what the article is worth. Although it does not happen very often, there are, however, some bargains to be had. At local salerooms it is often possible to buy furnishing pieces from China, India and the Balkans very cheaply as fine rug dealers have little interest in these. Apart from this cheap end of the market it is advisable not to venture without expert help.

One-off auctions Apart from long-established auctioneers with permanent premises and regular sales, there is another section of the profession which specializes in one-off sales held in hired premises — usually hotel ballrooms or public halls. Some of these sales are of ill-repute: a sale is preceded by a colourful advertising campaign in the local and national press which generally mentions cancelled export orders and goods stopped in transit, etc. Rugs are described in extravagant terms, and the sale is designed to catch the unwary, innocent and greedy public by encouraging them to bid excessive prices against bogus competition provided by the auctioneer's assistants. The goods on offer are likely to have been obtained on sale or return from the nearest wholesale warehouse, and to be of no particular merit. If in doubt, stay away.

Buying privately The main problem with buying privately is to fix a fair price in a situation in which neither the seller nor the buyer has any specialist knowledge. Unless expert advice is obtained from a specialized rug dealer, for example, many private individuals will have no idea what to ask and what to pay. Consequently, recently purchased modern rugs can be sold too dearly and antique pieces too cheaply.

For the buyer answering a small advertisement in a newspaper there is another pitfall: a high proportion of advertisers will be dealers or dealers' friends trying to dispose of modern rugs at inflated prices. Other vendors will be private individuals seeking to obtain the equivalent of their last insurance valuation, still others may be thieves disposing of stolen goods. As with the disreputable auction houses there are telltale signs: beware of such phrases as 'unwanted inheritance' or 'unwanted gift'. Always seek advice before parting with a large sum of money and ask to see evidence that the vendor has a proper title to the goods.

A last word on buying If you don't know about oriental rugs, you *must* know your dealer.

Selling Oriental Rugs

Rug owners sell for a variety of reasons, for example, when an estate is wound up, when moving to a smaller house or when cash is needed. There are different ways of selling rugs, some better than others.

When selling, the first step is to find out approximately what the rug in question is worth. To do this you can get a valuation from a dealer or an auctioneer, or free information can be obtained by taking the rug to a saleroom and asking advice 'with a view to sale'. But if the saleroom's rug expert does not happen to be on hand, you may receive an unreliable estimate. A previous insurance valuation is likely to be misleading; if out of date it will be too low; if recent, it is likely to be too high. With a rough idea of the worth of your piece you have the choice of selling privately, selling

to a dealer – either outright or on commission – or selling through a saleroom.

Selling privately Placing a newspaper advertisement in your local paper and waiting to see who comes to your house can be a traumatic experience. Dealers will call but will be interested only in buying cheaply; private buyers will be ignorant of values and will tend to waste your time, and you run the very real risk of attracting the attention of potential burglars. This method is not recommended.

Selling to a dealer Talk again to your local dealer and ask if he is interested in buying your piece. He will prefer you to state the price you require, and if you do he will either accept it or, more likely, make you an offer. You can either accept his offer, or say that you wish to obtain a competitive offer from other dealers. If your piece has special merit or is of high value, it is worth obtaining a number of different offers, preferably from dealers in a different area. Remember that a dealer's first offer will not usually be his highest and that sometimes a certain amount of haggling is accepted in the rug trade.

An alternative approach, particularly if you are sure of the value of the piece and do not require the cash urgently, is to leave it for sale on commission with the dealer. You will get a better price this way.

Selling at auction Selling at auction is the most satisfactory method of disposing of pieces that are rare and difficult to value, or are of high value. Such pieces are best tested in the competitive market place which the saleroom provides. Goods should be taken to the auctioneer well before the sale date – about four weeks locally and up to three months for the international auctions. The vendor will receive a copy of the catalogue of the sale and will be asked to agree a reserve price, if any, which is the price below which the rug will not be allowed to be sold. If the rug does not reach its reserve price, it will be 'bought in' by the auctioneer and either returned to the vendor or re-offered in a later sale. An unsold commission will be charged to the vendor and although this is variable, it can be anything between five to ten per cent of the reserve price.

When the rug is re-offered, it will usually be at a lower reserve price and — because the trade will recognize it — it will rarely reach the same price level as on its first appearance. In advising a reserve price, the auctioneer will tend to err on the low side (because it is in his interests to achieve a sale); equally, vendors must guard against being greedy by setting an unrealistically high reserve, on their rugs before the sale.

It is a common fallacy that the grand international auction houses will always achieve better prices than the local houses. The psychology of the saleroom is complex. The number of lots and the choice available in an international auction house is vast; there will be a feeling that each piece on offer will have been 'seen' by the whole world and its attractiveness thus marginally diminished. On the other hand, a local saleroom may have only one valuable piece among the rug lots. It will look outstandingly desirable among a collection of nondescript rugs, whereas at an international house it would be keeping company with a dozen other such pieces, of which three might be superior. In a local sale the rug is put up; competition is vigorous as the trade has made a long journey for that one piece; the private buyer competes against the trade; the ring dealers are determined not to let the non-ring dealers succeed; finally, the piece is sold to an independent dealer for a far higher price than in a major city.

Aside from this illustration, it is probably true that ordinary and good 'commercial' pieces sell as well or better in the local salerooms, while rare collectors' or 'museum' pieces, and very expensive rugs attracting an international clientele, will do better in an international saleroom.

After the sale, if successful, you will receive an advice note listing prices realized. About one month later you will receive a cheque for the net proceeds — the sale price less the auctioneers' commission (usually ten per cent where a buyer's premium is also charged) and less insurance charges and, in some countries, capital transfer taxes or value added tax on the commission.

Selling to advertisers

Many advertisers seek to buy oriental rugs by claiming to offer the best prices and a free valuation. Often these potential purchasers are merely bargain hunters looking for innocent, ignorant rug owners to fall into their trap. My advice in this situation would be never to send a rug to an advertiser whom you don't know, no matter how large or impressive his advertisement. Similarly, one should never invite a strange advertiser to one's home or sell a rug to a stranger without a sound second opinion as to its value. Once you are satisfied as to the value of your rug, you should never part with it to a stranger without receiving the full amount of money for it in cash.

Valuation and Insurance

Most oriental rug owners, like lovers of other arts, view their art form primarily as an object of aesthetic pleasure, its value taking second place; yet a feeling of contentment comes with the realization that beautiful things around the home also have an investment value. For mundane purposes a strictly monetary value can be attributed to such works of art. For insuring oriental rugs and for probate or family division, a professional valuation or appraisal is an absolute necessity.

Where to Obtain an Oriental Rug Valuation

Professional valuation is a highly skilled and specialized task which comparatively few people are qualified to undertake. Correct identification of a rug, as well as a detailed knowledge of prices and the market are required, in order to give a realistic valuation for whatever purpose. A satisfactory valuation of an oriental rug is unlikely to be obtained from an antique dealer or a general country auctioneer. Even a licensed appraiser would have difficulty in assessing the value. Most of these people cover a wide spectrum of items in the general world of art from silver to furniture and paintings. They would freely admit that they do not have the necessary experience which comes from the daily handling of rugs, nor the time to devote to absorbing the pertinent information concerning the fluctuating oriental rug market.

For a correct valuation, the rug owner must seek out an authority with extensive knowledge in the field. Either a reputable rug dealer or a firm of auctioneers holding regular specialist rug sales with rug experts on their staff or on call, should be approached. The importance of obtaining a valuation from an experienced and professional party cannot be overstated. Valuations can be made at the valuer's premises or, by prior arrangement, at a location designated by the owner.

Valuation Fees

Payment for the services of a valuer varies from company to company. Some companies work on a flat fee basis, quoting a fixed amount to carry out the valuation. Others prefer to receive a percentage of the valuation figure given. When a rug has been purchased from a rug dealer, the valuation may even be given without charge as a service to the client. It is naturally advisable to check the fee basis prior to appointing a valuer.

The percentages charged for a written valuation usually depend on the amount involved in the final valuation. As a general guide, the lower the value, the higher the fee; the higher the value, the lower the fee. Where a small amount is involved, the valuation fee is normally two per cent of the total value of the rugs, whereas on a sizeable collection of valuable rugs, the percentage would probably be one per cent of the total value. It is unlikely that a percentage based fee would drop below one per cent to a person who is not in the trade.

Factors Affecting the Value of Oriental Rugs

Valuation is not a hit-or-miss affair; it is a methodical appraisal of the various components which go to make up a value, adjusted at the end by the valuer's flair and feel for the subject and his knowledge of the current state of the market.

The following basic factors are taken into consideration when any simple appraisal or valuation is being undertaken:

a Origin

b Size and shape, uniformity as a whole, runner, square footage or unusual size

c Quality of make, fineness of knotting, type and quality of pile

d Design and execution – outstanding artistic merit and design

e Colours and dyes – vegetable, or synthetic dyes; balance of colour

f Age – whether antique, semi-antique, new

g Rarity

h Condition – possible wear or damage

i Market situation – current price levels being reached for comparable items

j Overall impression – amalgamation of all points and balanced conclusion drawn.

These factors are similar to those taken into account when purchasing a rug.

As there are no two rugs exactly the same, there are no absolutely set rules to follow: therefore, all valuations are expressed as the considered opinion of the valuer. It is possible that valuations from two recognized experts for the same item may differ because of the uniqueness of the product. The differences would, however, be fractional.

Valuation for Probate and Family Division

A professional valuation is needed when the owner of oriental rugs dies, in order to establish the values to be distributed to the beneficiaries of his estate. Capital transfer taxes (if any) will also be based on this given value and government revenue departments are likely to insist on a specialist valuation if the chattels of the estate are thought to be of a significant value. Similarly, a formal valuation is often needed in the case of a separation or divorce settlements or on the setting up of family trusts.

The basis of valuation for these purposes is the valuer's estimate of the net proceeds of the sale of the rugs on the open market, after selling expenses have been deducted. In practice, this means the estimated selling price to a dealer or public auction, less the auctioneer's fee and incidental expenses like transport and special advertising.

Valuation for Insurance

Oriental rugs, like jewellery, paintings and other works of art, require to be insured against possible damage or loss by fire, theft and other risks. Rug loss or damage can be catastrophic when the item concerned is not properly covered by the insurance policy, especially with the continuing escalating price trend.

Most insurance companies place a limit on the value that may be attributed to any individual item among the overall contents insured. Over and above this specified figure (which may be a set figure or a percentage of the total cover), a list of individual items and their values is necessary. To back such a list of values, a professional appraisal by a skilled expert is looked for by the insurance company. This is required for the cover of oriental rugs, particularly in the case of antique rugs where values for unique pieces are not easily established. Unless the item is backed by such expert appraisal, the insurers are unlikely to pay the full amount claimed, and previously covered, in the event of loss. In short, oriental rugs (unless of minimal value) usually cannot be properly insured under general cover or under a blanket policy. However, it is important to discuss this point with your insurance adviser.

The basis for valuation for insurance purposes differs from that adopted for valuation for probate or family division. It is the valuer's estimate of what it would cost the owner at full retail price (plus current purchase taxes where relevant) to replace the rug with one of equivalent type, quality, age, size, condition and rarity on the ordinary retail market. It represents a current replacement value.

A written valuation should be updated in accordance with basic inflation every year. However, the item needs to be revalued every three to five years by an expert as the price of oriental rugs is rising rapidly (some rugs more so than others) and the market is constantly changing.

How to Insure Oriental Rugs

Insurance is a wide and sometimes complex field and an insurance broker is perhaps the most knowledgeable person to advise with regard to the coverage of oriental rugs. As a guide, there are basically three types of home owner's insurance policies:

  a Coverage against specified risks (including fire, theft, malicious damage, water damage and other similar contingencies

  b Cover as outlined in **a**, plus all forms of accidental damage

  c All risks cover (including damage) which provides for coverage outside the usual location of items insured

Obviously item **c** provides the most complete cover and this is most desirable for oriental rugs. However, damage by vermin (moths, beetles and so forth) and general wear and tear are obviously not covered.

The maximum amount payable for any one item by the insurance company should be clarified with the broker. If the value of the rugs is over this limit, which in most cases it will be, advise your broker of the details (size, type and value) relating to each rug and he will secure the cover. This can be arranged over the telephone, provided supporting documents (a professional valuation or, in the event of a new purchase, a copy of the purchase invoice) are sent shortly after. Informing the insurance company of specific valuable items does not necessarily increase the insurance premium payment, but does ensure that full and complete cover is provided.

Insurance brokers always stress the need to insure accurately and this applies particularly in the case of oriental rugs. To over-insure your rugs results in the unnecessary payment of a higher premium; to under-insure them is probably worse, for the cost of replacing or repairing a rug is constantly escalating.

How to Claim from an Insurance Company

The processing of a claim for loss or damage to an oriental rug is much the same as for any other type of claim. As soon as any damage or loss occurs, the insurance broker should be contacted and informed of the circumstances. The broker will forward a claim form for completion with the required information. This form will then be processed by the insurance company and the client subsequently compensated.

When the damage is minor and the cost of repair or replacement minimal, companies will often pay the amount claimed without further evidence having to be submitted. When the figure being claimed is more sizeable, it is usual for the insurance company's adjuster to visit the insured party personally to inspect the damage. In the case of oriental rugs, the adjuster may rely on a reputable dealer for guidance if he (the adjuster) does not have the specialized knowledge needed. The adjuster will realistically assess the extent of damage or loss and confirm or dispute the claim. Insurance companies are usually sympathetic and fair but, in the unlikely event that the client is unhappy with the recommended amount being offered by way of compensation by the insurance company, an independent assessor can be appointed by the client who will give a second opinion and act on your behalf to reach a necessary agreement with the adjuster.

The Valuation Certificate and Photographic Record

All valuations prepared for formal purposes should be in writing and issued on the valuer's official letter head. Three copies should be prepared: one for the client, one for the client's insurance company, and one to be kept by the valuer. The valuation should be dated and should state the location and the ownership of the rugs. Each rug should be described individually in sufficient detail to establish its distinguishing characteristics and its general condition.

It is vital that a colour photographic record of each rug is kept, in addition to the valuation. This is particularly important in the case of rugs with a high value. Photographs may be taken by a professional photographer, or the valuer or owner and even the most amateur photograph is better than none at all. A photographic record is essential in the unfortunate case of theft, as it can be circulated by the police to all parts of the world if necessary, and the chances of locating the stolen goods will be much improved. For added protection, and in anticipation of fire damage, it is advisable to keep a duplicate valuation and photograph of each rug at a location other than that at which the rugs are situated — a safe or bank vault is ideal.

*A late nineteenth-century Senneh rug (6 ft
8 in×4 ft 5 in/202 cm×132.7 cm) with an
exposed centre medallion on an ivory field and
densely patterned spandrels.*

Appendix:
Where to Learn More about Oriental Rugs

Oriental Rug Societies

The aims of the oriental rug and textile societies which are developing in many parts of the world, are to provide meeting places for local enthusiasts and to stimulate interest in the subject by providing programmes of lectures, practical demonstrations and group visits to important exhibitions and lectures. As such societies are not usually widely publicized, a fully international list for the use of potential members is given here for the first time.

Australia

The Oriental Rug Society of
New South Wales
512 Cleveland Street
Surrey Hill
New South Wales

Canada

The Oriental Rug Society Inc
120 Stibbard Avenue
Toronto
Ontario M4P 2C2

Denmark

Orientalsk Taeppeklub
c/o Werner Albrecht
Hovsmedevej 5
DK 3400
Hilleroed

Hungary

The Hungarian Oriental Carpet Club
c/o A. Nagykaldi
H-1112
Dorozsami u. 31
Budapest

Switzerland

Freunde des Orientteppichs Basel
c/o Herr R. J. Graf
Rheingasse 31
Postfach 4005
Basel

United Kingdom

The Oriental Rug and Textile
Society of Great Britain
c/o Mrs Jill Hobsbawn
75 Nottingham Terrace
London NW1

United States

Hajji Baba Club International
Jeff Boucher
c/o Dolores Cox
7404 Valley Crest Boulevard
Annandale
Virginia 22003

The Chicago Rug Society
c/o Bette Caracci (Secretary)
644 Bellefort Avenue
Oak Park
Chicago
Illinois 60302

The New York Rug Society
c/o Sarah H. Sherill
Magazine Antiques
551 Fifth Avenue
New York
New York 10021

The Armenian Rug Society
c/o Dr Viken Sassouni
607 Washington Road
Pittsburgh
Pennsylvania 15228

The Pittsburg Rug Society
c/o George O'Bannon
1129 Whightman Street
Pittsburgh
Pennsylvania.15217

The Rochester Rug Society
c/o Nancy Hallowell
12 Washington Avenue
Pittsford
New York 14534

The Princeton Rug Society
c/o D. N. Wilber
50 Wilson Road
Princeton
New Jersey 08540

The Eastern Rug Society
c/o Mr O'Dell
PO Box 968
Richmond
Virginia 23207

Hajji Baba Club
15 East Pierrepont Avenue
Rutherford
New Jersey 07070

The St Louis Rug Society
c/o Helen Longmire
340 Papin Avenue
St Louis
Minnesota 63119

West Germany

Freundeskreis orientalischer
Teppiche und Textilien in Westfalen
Bahlmannstrasse 12
Munster 4400

Museums

Many museums and galleries throughout the world hold noteworthy collections of oriental rugs and textiles which travellers with an interest in the subject might like to visit. The following guide lists the small number of specialist museums whose sole concern is rugs and textiles, as well as the major institutions whose oriental rug collections are particularly distinguished.

Austria

Austrian Museum of Applied Arts
Stubenring 5
1010 Vienna 1

Museum fur Volkerkunde
Neue Hofburg Heldenplatz
Vienna 1000

Canada

Royal Ontario Museum
100 Queens Park
Toronto
Ontario 415

Denmark

David Samling
(C. L. David's Collection)
30 Kronprinsessegade
Copenhagen K

Det Danske Kunstindustrimuseum
(Museum of Decorative Art)
Bredgade 68
Copenhagen K

East Germany

Staatliche Museen zu Berlin
Islamische Museum
(Pergamon Museum)
Boderstrasse 1–3
East Berlin

Egypt

Egyptian National Museum
Midan-el-Tahrir
Kasr El-Nil
Cairo

France

Musée Historique des Tissus
34 rue de la Charité
Lyon 69002

Musée des Arts Décoratifs (Union
Centrale des Arts Décoratifs)
107–109 rue de Rivoli
Palais du Louvre
Pavillon de Marsan
Paris 75001

Musée National du Louvre
Palais du Louvre
Pavillon Mollien
Place de Carrousel
Paris 75001

Greece

Benaki Museum
1 Koumbari Street
Athens

Holland

Rijksmuseum Amsterdam
Stadhouderskade 42
Amsterdam 1000

Hungary

Museum of Applied Arts
Üllöi út 33–37
Budapest 10

India

Calico Museum of Textiles
Ahmedabad
Gujarat

Israel

L.A. Mayer Memorial Institute for
Islamic Art
2 Palmach Street
Jerusalem

Italy

Museo Bardini e Galleria Corsim
piazza dei Mozzi 1a
Florence 50100

Museo Nazionale del Bargello
via del Proconsolo 4
Florence 50100

Museo Poldi Pezzoli
via Manzoni 12
Milan 20100

Portugal

Calouste Gulbenkian Museum
Avenida Antonio Augusto de Aguiar
Lisbon

Spain

Insituto de Valencia de Don Juan
Calle Fortuny 43
Madrid

Sweden

Göteborgs Etnografiska Museum
(Ethnographical Museum)
Norra Museum
Norra Hamnagatan 12
Göteborg 40090

Nationalmuseum
Södra Blasieholmshamnen
Stockholm

Switzerland

Seminar fur Völkskunde
Augustinergasse 19
4051 Basel

Thyssen-Bornemisza Collection
Villa Favorita
Castagnola
Ticino

Museum Rietberg
Gablerstrasse 15
Zurich

Turkey

Ethnological Museum
Talat Pasa Boulevard
Ankara

Museum for Turkish and Islamic Art
Süleymaniye
Istanbul

Topkapi Saray
Sultanahmed
Istanbul

Vaklifar Museum
Sultanahmed
Istanbul

Mevlãna Museum
Konya

United Kingdom

Fitzwilliam Museum
Trumpington Street
Cambridge CB2 1RB

Burrell Collection
Camphill Museum
Queen's Park
Glasgow G41 2EW
Scotland

Victoria & Albert Museum
South Kensington
London SW7 2RC

Whitworth Art Gallery
University of Manchester
Manchester M15 6ER

United States

Walters Art Gallery
600 N. Charles Street
Baltimore 21201

Museum of Fine Arts
465 Huntingdon Avenue
Boston
Massachusetts 02115

Fogg Art Museum
Harvard University
Quincy Street
Cambridge
Massachusetts

The Art Institute of Chicago
Michigan Avenue at Adams Street
Chicago
Illinois 60603

County Museum of Art
5905 Wilshire Boulevard
Los Angeles
California 90038

Museum of Art
11150 East Boulevard
Cleveland
Ohio 44106

Henry Francis du Pont Winterthur
Museum
Delaware 19735

Detroit Institute of Arts
5200 Woodward Avenue
Detroit 48202

School of Art
Museum of Fine Arts
1001 Bissonnet Street
PO Box 6826
Houston 77005

Williams Rockhill Nelson Gallery &
Mary Atkins Museum of Fine Arts
4525 Oak Street
Kansas City
Missouri 64111

J. Paul Getty Museum
17985 Pacific Coast Highway
Malibu 90265

The Newark Museum
43–49 Washington Street
Newark
New Jersey

Brooklyn Museum
188 Eastern Parkway
New York
New York 11238

Frick Collection
1 E 70th Street
New York
New York 10021

Hispanic Society of America
115th Street at Broadway
New York
New York 10032

The Metropolitan Museum of Art
(Department of Western European
Art)
5th Avenue at 82nd Street
New York City
New York 10028

The Allen Memorial Art Museum
Oberlin College
Oberlin
Ohio 44074

Philadelphia Museum of Art
Benjamin Franklin Parkway
Box 7646
Philadelphia 19101

Fine Arts Museum of San Francisco
MH de Young Memorial Museum
San Francisco
California

Palace of the Legion of Honor
Lincoln Park
San Francisco 94100

St. Louis Art Museum
Forest Park
St. Louis
Missouri 63110

The Textile Museum
2320 S. Street N.W.
Washington DC 20008

USSR

State Fine Art Museum of the
Republic of Turkmenistan
Pr. Svobody 84
Ashkhabad
Turkmenistan

Museum of Ethnography
Baku
Azerbaijan

Museum of Ethnography
Erevan
Armenia

Hermitage Museum
M. Dvortsovaya naberezhnaya 34
Leningrad

National Museum of Ethnography of
the Peoples of the USSR
Inzhenernaya ul. 4/1
Leningrad

Museum of Oriental Art
Ul. Obukha 16
Moscow

Samarkand National Museum
Svoetskaya ul. 51
Smarkand
Uzbekistan

Museum of Applied Art
Ul. Spulvkova 11
Tashkent
Uzbekistan

National Art Museum of Uzbekistan
Ul. Gogolya 1M
Tashkent
Uzbekistan

West Germany

Museum fur Islamische Kunst
Dept. of Islamic Art & Antiquities)
Lansstrasse 8
Berlin 1000

Museum fur Völkerkunde
Lansstrasse 8
Berlin 1000

Museum fur Ostasiatische Kunst
Hahnentorburg
Rudolfplatz
Cologne 5000

Statliche Museum fur Völkerkunde
(State Museum of Ethnography)
Maximilianstrasse 42
Munich 8000

Museum fur Kunsthandwerk
(Museum of Applied Arts)
Schaumainkai 15
Hessen
Frankfurt 6000

Museum fur Kunst und Gewerbe
Steintorplatz
Hamburg 2001

Hamburgisches Museum fur
Völkerkunde
Binderstrasse 14
Hamburg 2014

Kestner-Museum
Trammplatz 3
Hannover 3000

Museen fur Kunst und
Kulturgeschichte der Hansestadt
Lubeck (Ethnography Collection)
Duvekenstrasse 21
Lubeck 2400

Bayerisches Nationalmuseum
(Bavarian National Museum)
Prinzregentenstrasse 3
Munich 8000

Specialist Publications
At present there is only one journal,
Hali, which is totally devoted to the
scholarly study of the history and
techniques of oriental rugs. It is an
internationally orientated quarterly
which has offices in London and
Philadelphia. *Hali* is sold by sub-
scription and further information can
be obtained from:

Robert Pinner & Michael Franses
Managing Editors
*Hali – The International Journal of
Oriental Carpets and Textiles*
193a Shirland Road
London W9
Tel: 01-286-1889

Dennis R. Dodds
US Editor *Hali*
PO Box 4312
Philadelphia PA 19118
USA
Tel: 215-843-3090

Acknowledgments

Author's Acknowledgments
I owe heartfelt thanks to all the learned friends and
associates who generously contributed their time and
knowledge to help me complete this technically complex
book.

That it took a long time to prepare was due, in part,
to my attempt to ensure clear and accurate descriptions
of the apparently simple processes in repairing oriental
rugs, the preservation and maintenance of which are
my special concern and my life's work.

The many months of labour necessary to achieve the
completion of the text were shared with Charlotte
Smallman who was more than instrumental in helping
me to find the right words to interpret my ideas. Her
sympathetic understanding of the subject and dedica-
tion to its proper presentation, allied with her forbearing
patience, made the production of this book possible.
For this she has my lasting gratitude.

The publishers would like to thank many private collectors for providing illustrations for this book and also the
following for providing the illustrations on the pages
listed below:

Christie's: 28 left; Jean-Paul Froget: 110–111; Leo
Hilber/Office du Livre, Fribourg: 22, 34, 47; India Office
Library and Records: 16; M. Konieczny: 19, 48;
National Gallery: 14; National Trust: 58–59 (John
Bethel), 60 (Jon Gibson); Novosti: 13; Bury Peerless: 7,
10–11; Sotheby Parke Bernet & Co: 28, 31, 49, 50;
Victoria and Albert Museum: 15, 52; Elizabeth Whiting:
62–63; Ian Adam: 113. Drawings: Jill Shipley.

Studio photography by Paul Williams: 38 top, 38 bottom,
40, 42, 54–55, 66, 69 left, 69 right, 70, 72, 75 top, 75
bottom, 79, 83, 86, 88, 89 left, 89 right, 90, 92, 94, 95,
98, 99 left, 99 right, 101 left, 101 right, 107 left, 107
right; David Quick: 90; Dennis Waugh: 35.

Index

Figures in *italics* refer to pages in which
illustrations occur